Perfect Food
PERFECT HEALTH

Front cover: Roasted Garlic Pesto Pizza, page 73; photography by Howard L. Puckett; styling by Melanie J. Clarke; recipe developed by Niccole Davis

Editor: **Alyson Moreland Haynes**
Art Director: **Amy Heise**
Managing Editor: **Kay Fuston**
Senior Writer: **Kate Neale Cooper**
Assistant Food Editor: **Joe Watts**
Copy Editors: **Maria Parker Hopkins, Carol Boker**
Production Manager: **Liz Rhoades**
Copy/Production Assistant: **Kate McWhorter**
Food Interns: **Niccole Davis, Keetha DePriest**
Art Intern: **Robbie Morgan**
Copy Intern: **Jennifer Wegman**

Recipe Developers: **Elizabeth Tyler Luckett, Julia Dowling Rutland, Elizabeth Taliaferro**
Photographers: **Ralph Anderson, Jim Bathie, Tina Cornett, Colleen Duffley, Becky Luigart-Stayner, Randy Mayor, Howard L. Puckett**
Photo Stylists: **Cindy Manning Barr, Kay E. Clarke, Melanie J. Clarke, Virginia R. Cravens, Mary Catherine Muir, Fonda Shaia, Ashley J. Wyatt**

Weight Watchers Magazine Test Kitchen Director: **Kathleen Phillips;**
Assistant Director: **Gayle Hayes Sadler;** Staff: **Julie Christopher, Natalie E. King, L. Victoria Knowles, Jan A. Smith**

Editor, *Weight Watchers* Magazine: **Kate Greer**
Art Director: **Jamie Ezra Mark**
Articles Editor: **Matthew Solan**
Editorial Coordinator: **Christine O'Connell**

Senior Vice President, Publisher: **Jeffrey C. Ward**
General Manager: **Thomas C. Marshall**
Business Manager: **Michael W. Stern**
Marketing Manager: **Betsey Hummel**
Production Manager: **Brent Kizzire**
Assistant Production Manager: **Robin Boteler**

President and CEO: **Tom Angelillo**
Executive Vice President: **Bruce Akin**
Executive Vice President: **Scott Sheppard**
Vice President, Administration: **Jeanetta Keller**
Vice President, Consumer Marketing: **Hallett Johnson III**
Vice President, Circulation: **Pat Vander Meer**
Vice President, Magazine Production: **Larry Rinehart**
Vice President, Finance: **Bruce Larson**

Back cover: Almond Crème Caramel, page 68; photography by Howard L. Puckett; styling by Melanie J. Clarke

WELCOME

The Food Pyramid has become synonymous with nutrition in this country. Sure, it's a great visual aid, but do we really understand how to put its philosophy into practice? Many of us could draw the food pyramid with our eyes closed, but we're still falling woefully short of making wise food choices. Here's help. Although it contains more than 125 recipes, *Perfect Food, Perfect Health* is more than a cookbook. It's an introduction to the health benefits of some of nature's most powerful and flavorful foods. In the pages of this book, you'll find all the information and inspiration you need to try something new, from tips on shopping and storage to original recipes and helpful step-by-step photographs.

And as far as the food pyramid is concerned, stop focusing on the numbers and start thinking about what they represent. That's what the Departments of Agriculture and Health and Human Services did when they wrote "Dietary Guidelines for America," seven simple, sensible suggestions. Think of them as the Cliff's Notes of nutrition, the food pyramid in plain English.

1. Eat a variety of foods. Milk supplies plenty of calcium, but no iron; meat's got iron, but no calcium. The point is that no single food can supply all the nutrients you need, so shake it up.

2. Balance the food you eat with physical activity. A *Weight Watchers* Magazine reader expressed this concept best when she explained, "I approach my meal plan the very same way that I balance my checkbook. I apportion a certain number of meals and calories per day, and if I exceed that amount, I tell myself that I have to exercise more."

3. Eat plenty of fruits, vegetables, and grain products. Most of the calories in your diet should come from these three food groups because they're plant foods, which are low in calories and high in fiber and complex carbohydrates.

4. Eat foods that are low in fat, saturated fat, and cholesterol. Our bodies need fat. But not all fat is created equal. No more than 10% of your daily calories should come from saturated fat (and no more than 30% should come from total fat). Eating fewer animal products, which is the only source of dietary cholesterol, will help you lower the cholesterol and fat in your diet.

5. Use sugars only in moderation. Ever hear the term "empty calories"?

6. Avoid adding salt and sodium to food. Sure salt contains sodium and chloride, which are both essential nutrients, but you're getting plenty without ever touching that shaker on your kitchen table.

7. Drink alcohol in moderation, if you drink it at all. What's "moderate"? One drink a day for a woman, two drinks a day for a man. What's one drink? 12 ounces of beer, 5 ounces of wine, 1½ ounces of 80-proof distilled spirits.

Eating well doesn't get any easier than that.

Alyson M. Haynes

Perfect Food

PERFECT HEALTH

c o n t e n t s

Good-for-You Grains

It's no coincidence that *America the Beautiful* salutes our "amber waves of grain." A culinary staple, grains helped form society and can do an impressive number on your eating habits as well.

O*nce our hunter-gatherer ancestors discovered that wheat and barley could be planted, grown, and harvested, they no longer had to roam in search for food, and could finally settle in one place. It's no wonder then, that in Japan the mythic figure that represents abundance and prosperity is known as the Great Grain Spirit. Unfortunately, Americans place grains a tad lower on the importance scale. According to the FDA's Food Guide Pyramid, grains should be the foundation of a healthy diet. And although it is the only food category Americans have eaten more of over the past 10 years, we still don't get enough. A recent Gallup survey found that Americans eat 3.2 servings of grains a day, well below the recommended 6 to 11 servings. Why so many? Because much of the hype is true: Grains are credited with everything from reducing the risk of heart disease and some cancers to lowering total and "bad" cholesterol levels. Plus, grains are low in fat and rich in fiber, complex carbohydrates, vitamins, minerals, and protein. And so that you get the variety you need, we've used more than 10 different grains to create recipes such as Couscous-and-Feta Cakes, Barley-and-Mushroom Casserole, and Streusel Oatmeal Cake. The Great Grain Spirit is surely smiling.*

Barley-and-Black Bean Salad and a cold glass of lemonade make a refreshing meal.

Pair Couscous-and-Feta
Cakes with a salad
of cucumbers,
tomatoes, kalamata
olives, and lemon.

Barley-and-Black Bean Salad

3 · cups cooked pearl barley
2 cups drained canned black beans
1½ cups frozen whole-kernel corn, thawed
1½ cups diced tomato
1 cup frozen green peas, thawed
1 cup peeled chopped ripe avocado
¼ cup chopped fresh cilantro
½ teaspoon salt
¼ teaspoon pepper
½ cup water
2 tablespoons fresh lemon juice
1 tablespoon grated fresh onion
1 tablespoon vegetable oil
2 garlic cloves, minced
Romaine lettuce leaves
18 (¼-inch-thick) slices peeled ripe avocado
18 (¼-inch-thick) wedges tomato
9 lemon wedges

1. Combine first 9 ingredients in a large bowl, and toss gently. Combine water and next 4 ingredients in a small bowl; stir with a whisk until well blended. Pour over barley mixture, and toss gently. Spoon onto lettuce-lined plates using a slotted spoon. Garnish with avocado, tomato, and lemon wedges. Serve salad at room temperature. Yield: 9 servings (serving size: 1 cup salad, 2 avocado slices, and 2 tomato wedges).

POINTS: 4; **Exchanges:** 2½ Starch, 1 Fat
Per serving: CAL 244 (26% from fat); PRO 8.7g; FAT 7.1g (sat 1.2g); CARB 40.3g; FIB 8.2g; CHOL 0mg; IRON 2.5mg; SOD 267mg; CALC 37mg

Couscous-and-Feta Cakes

An electric skillet or griddle works well for this recipe because there's more room for the cakes. Otherwise, use a nonstick skillet, and cook in batches. They're delicious plain or served with marinara sauce.

2½ cups water
1 cup uncooked couscous
4 teaspoons olive oil, divided
1 cup minced red onion
1 cup minced red bell pepper
½ cup minced green bell pepper

2 garlic cloves, minced
1 (4-ounce) package crumbled feta cheese
½ cup all-purpose flour
½ cup egg substitute
2 tablespoons minced fresh parsley
¼ teaspoon salt
¼ teaspoon white pepper

1. Bring water to a boil in a small saucepan; stir in couscous. Remove from heat; cover and let stand 5 minutes. Fluff with a fork.

2. Place 1 teaspoon oil in an electric skillet; heat to 375°. Add onion, bell peppers, and garlic; sauté 5 minutes. Combine couscous, onion mixture, cheese, and next 5 ingredients in a large bowl; stir well.

3. Place ½ teaspoon oil in skillet; heat to 375°. Place ⅓ cup couscous mixture for each of 4 portions into skillet, shaping each portion into a 3-inch cake in the skillet. Cook 6 minutes or until golden brown, turning cakes carefully after 3 minutes. Remove cakes from skillet; set aside, and keep warm. Repeat procedure with remaining oil and couscous mixture. Yield: 12 servings (serving size: 2 cakes).

POINTS: 5; **Exchanges:** 2 Starch, 1 Fat, ½ Med-fat Meat
Per serving: CAL 242 (28% from fat); PRO 10g; FAT 7.6g (sat 3.2g); CARB 34g; FIB 2.4g; CHOL 16mg; IRON 2.2mg; SOD 344mg; CALC 112mg

New Orleans Dirty Quinoa

Rinsing quinoa before cooking removes saponin, a naturally occurring soaplike substance on the outside of the grain. If you don't have a sieve fine enough to restrain this tiny grain, use cheesecloth to line the sieve.

3 cups uncooked quinoa
1 tablespoon olive oil
4 ounces chicken livers, finely chopped
½ pound chopped lean Canadian bacon
1 cup chopped onion
¾ cup diced celery
½ cup diced green bell pepper
2 tablespoons chopped shallots
2 large garlic cloves, minced
1 bay leaf
⅓ cup water
1 tablespoon Worcestershire sauce
2 teaspoons Creole seasoning

¼ teaspoon hot sauce
2 (14¼-ounce) cans fat-free chicken broth
½ cup sliced green onions

1. Place quinoa in a fine sieve; rinse under cold water. Drain; set aside.

2. Heat oil in a large saucepan over medium-low heat. Add chicken livers; sauté 4 minutes or until done. Add bacon and next 6 ingredients; sauté 3 minutes or until vegetables are crisp-tender. Add quinoa; cook 2 minutes, stirring constantly. Add ⅓ cup water and next 4 ingredients; bring to a boil. Reduce heat, and simmer, uncovered, 15 minutes or until liquid is absorbed, stirring occasionally. Remove from heat, and discard bay leaf. Stir in green onions. Yield: 8 servings (serving size: 1 cup).

Note: Look for the grain quinoa (KEEN-wah) next to the rice at large supermarkets or at nutrition stores.

POINTS: 6; **Exchanges:** 3½ Starch, 1 Lean Meat, ½ Fat
Per serving: CAL 344 (21% from fat); PRO 18.9g; FAT 8g (sat 1.4g); CARB 49.6g; FIB 9.5g; CHOL 76mg; IRON 7.6 mg; SOD 1,012mg; CALC 60mg

Streusel Oatmeal Cake With Caramel-Cranberry-Apple Sauce

This cake takes a little extra time to prepare, but the results are worth it.

1 cup regular oats
1 (8-ounce) carton vanilla low-fat yogurt
3 tablespoons stick margarine, softened
1 cup granulated sugar
1 large egg
¾ cup all-purpose flour
1 teaspoon baking powder
¼ teaspoon salt
1 cup finely chopped unpeeled Rome apple (about ½ pound)
1 teaspoon vanilla extract
Cooking spray
½ cup firmly packed brown sugar
¼ cup all-purpose flour
¼ cup regular oats
¼ teaspoon ground cinnamon

QUINOA

Quinoa is called the "super grain" because it comes closer than any other food to supplying all the nutrients needed to sustain life. It has more protein than any other grain, and it's higher in unsaturated fats but lower in carbohydrates than most grains. Quinoa also has a delicate, almost bland flavor like that of couscous.

Shopping

This grain is available at most health-food and specialty stores and at some supermarkets. It's available packaged or in bulk bins.

Storage

Quinoa can be stored in an airtight container for up to one year.

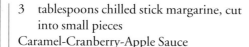

WHEAT BERRIES

Wheat berries are unprocessed, whole-wheat kernels minus the inedible hulls. After cooking them according to package directions, you can add wheat berries to salads, breads, hamburgers, and meat loaf.

Shopping
Look for wheat berries that are uniform in color with few undersized or broken kernels and few or none with husks attached.

Storage
Wheat berries can be stored for up to one year in an airtight container in a cool, dark, dry place.

3 tablespoons chilled stick margarine, cut into small pieces
Caramel-Cranberry-Apple Sauce

1. Preheat oven to 350°.

2. Place 1 cup oats in a food processor; process until finely ground. Set aside.

3. Spoon yogurt onto several layers of heavy-duty paper towels; spread to ½-inch thickness. Cover with additional paper towels; let stand 10 minutes. Scrape yogurt cheese into a bowl using a rubber spatula.

4. Combine yogurt cheese and 3 tablespoons softened margarine in a bowl; beat at medium speed of a mixer until blended. Gradually add granulated sugar, beating until light and fluffy. Add egg; beat just until blended.

5. Combine ground oats, flour, baking powder, and salt; stir well. Add to yogurt mixture, beating just until blended. Stir in unpeeled apple and vanilla. Spoon batter into a 9-inch square baking pan coated with cooking spray; set aside.

6. Combine brown sugar and next 3 ingredients; cut in chilled margarine with a pastry blender or 2 knives until mixture resembles coarse meal. Sprinkle evenly over batter. Bake at 350° for 40 minutes or until a wooden pick inserted in center comes out clean. Let cool on a wire rack. Serve with warm Caramel-Cranberry-Apple Sauce. Yield: 12 servings (serving size: 1 piece cake and 2 tablespoons sauce).

POINTS: 6; **Exchanges:** 2 Starch, 1½ Fruit, 1 Fat
Per serving: CAL 307 (22% from fat); PRO 4.2g; FAT 7.6g (sat 1.5g); CARB 56.4g; FIB 2.2g; CHOL 19mg; IRON 1.2mg; SOD 182mg; CALC 81mg

Caramel-Cranberry-Apple Sauce:

2 cups peeled chopped Rome apple (about 1 pound)
¾ cup apple juice
½ cup dried sweetened cranberries (such as Craisins)
10 small soft caramel candies

1. Combine first 3 ingredients in a small saucepan, and bring to a boil. Cover, reduce heat, and simmer 10 minutes. Remove apple and cranberries from juice using a slotted spoon; set fruit aside. Add caramel candies to juice, and cook over low heat until candies melt, stirring occasionally. Return fruit to caramel mixture. Serve warm. Yield: 1½ cups.

Barley-and-Mushroom Casserole
Instead of rice, try this easy, high-fiber side dish. It has a robust, nutty flavor.

1 (3½-ounce) package shiitake mushrooms
1 tablespoon stick margarine
1 (8-ounce) package presliced mushrooms
4 cups water
1 cup uncooked pearl barley
1 (1-ounce) envelope onion soup mix (such as Lipton Recipe Secrets)
Chopped fresh chives (optional)

1. Preheat oven to 350°.

2. Remove and discard stems from shiitake mushrooms; slice mushroom caps. Heat margarine in a medium nonstick skillet over medium-high heat. Add shiitake and presliced mushrooms; sauté 5 minutes or until tender. Set aside.

3. Combine water, barley, and onion soup mix in a 3-quart casserole; stir in mushroom mixture. Cover and bake at 350° for 1 hour and 15 minutes or until most of liquid is absorbed. Garnish with chives, if desired. Yield: 6 servings (serving size: about ¾ cup).

POINTS: 2; **Exchanges:** 2 Starch
Per serving: CAL 161 (14% from fat); PRO 4.4g; FAT 2.5g (sat 0.5g); CARB 31g; FIB 5.9g; CHOL 0mg; IRON 1.5mg; SOD 434mg; CALC 13mg

Southwestern Wheat Berry Pilaf

¾ cup uncooked wheat berries
2 (6-inch) Anaheim chiles
1 cup diced red bell pepper
1 cup peeled diced jicama
¾ cup minced red onion
⅓ cup minced fresh cilantro
3 tablespoons fresh lime juice
1½ tablespoons olive oil
½ teaspoon salt
2 garlic cloves, minced

1   (15-ounce) can black beans, rinsed and
    drained
Cilantro sprigs (optional)

1. Place wheat berries in a medium bowl; cover with water to 2 inches above wheat berries. Cover and let stand 8 hours. Drain.

2. Place wheat berries in a medium saucepan; cover with water to 2 inches above wheat berries, and bring to a boil. Reduce heat, and simmer, un-covered, 1 hour or until tender. Drain; set aside.

3. Cut chiles in half lengthwise; discard seeds and membranes. Place chile halves, skin side up, on a foil-lined baking sheet; flatten with hand. Broil chiles 8 minutes or until blackened. Place in a zip-top plastic bag; seal. Let stand 10 minutes. Peel and chop.

4. Combine chopped chiles, wheat berries, bell pepper, and next 8 ingredients in a large bowl; stir well. Serve chilled or at room temperature.

Garnish with cilantro sprigs, if desired. Yield: 6 servings (serving size: 1 cup).

Note: To save time on the day you serve this dish, you can soak the wheat berries the night before making the pilaf.

POINTS: 3; **Exchanges:** 2 Starch, ½ Fat
Per serving: CAL 190 (21% from fat); PRO 7.4g; FAT 4.4g (sat 0.6g); CARB 33g; FIB 6.2g; CHOL 0mg; IRON 1.6mg; SOD 309mg; CALC 27mg

Chile, Fresh Corn, and Grits Casserole

4   large Anaheim chiles (about 1 pound)
Cooking spray
1   teaspoon vegetable oil
1   cup fresh corn kernels (about 2 ears)
2   garlic cloves, minced
3   cups water
¾   cup uncooked regular grits
1   cup (4 ounces) shredded reduced-fat sharp cheddar cheese
1   teaspoon ground cumin

Tired of rice? Try our flavorful Southwestern Wheat Berry Pilaf.

Shrimp-and-Grits Gratin

½ teaspoon salt
¼ teaspoon black pepper
½ cup seeded chopped tomato
½ cup salsa
Cilantro sprigs (optional)

1. Place Anaheim chiles on a foil-lined baking sheet; broil 30 minutes or until blackened, turning after 15 minutes. Place in a zip-top plastic bag; seal bag, and let stand 15 minutes. Peel chiles, and discard stems, seeds, and membranes. Cut each chile lengthwise into 4 strips; set aside.

2. Preheat oven to 350°.

3. Coat a nonstick skillet with cooking spray; add oil, and place over medium heat until hot. Add corn; sauté until tender and lightly browned. Add garlic; sauté an additional 15 seconds. Remove from heat, and set aside.

4. Bring water to a boil in a medium saucepan. Gradually stir in grits; cover, reduce heat, and simmer 10 minutes or until thick, stirring occasionally. Add cheese and next 3 ingredients, stirring until cheese melts. Stir in corn mixture.

5. Spoon half of grits mixture into a 1-quart casserole coated with cooking spray. Arrange chile strips over grits mixture. Spoon remaining grits mixture over chiles. Bake, uncovered, at 350° for 25 minutes or until thoroughly heated (casserole will be soft and spoonable like grits).

6. Combine tomato and salsa; stir well. Spoon casserole into individual bowls; top with salsa mixture. Garnish with cilantro sprigs, if desired. Yield: 4 servings (serving size: ¾ cup casserole and ¼ cup salsa).

Note: Although it's hard to beat the flavor of fresh chiles and corn, you may prefer to streamline this recipe by using 4 (4-ounce) cans whole green chiles and 1 cup frozen whole-kernel corn, thawed. Remove the seeds from the drained canned chiles, and cut each one into 4 strips, as directed above.

POINTS: 4; **Exchanges:** 1½Starch, 1 Med-fat Meat, 1 Veg
Per serving: CAL 213 (32% from fat); PRO 12.6g; FAT 7.6g (sat 3.5g); CARB 27.4g; FIB 4.6g; CHOL 19mg; IRON 2.5mg; SOD 591mg; CALC 293mg

Shrimp-and-Grits Gratin

3 tablespoons chopped fresh or 3 teaspoons dried basil
2 tablespoons fresh lemon juice
1 tablespoon olive oil
1 tablespoon raspberry vinegar
1 teaspoon grated lemon rind
1 garlic clove, minced
1 pound medium shrimp, peeled and deveined
4 cups boiling water
3 cups uncooked instant grits
¼ cup grated Parmesan cheese, divided
2 tablespoons chopped fresh or 2 teaspoons dried parsley
1 teaspoon grated lemon rind
¼ teaspoon pepper
Cooking spray
⅛ teaspoon paprika
Basil sprigs (optional)

1. Combine first 7 ingredients in a large zip-top plastic bag; seal bag, and marinate in refrigerator 2 hours, turning bag occasionally. Remove shrimp from bag; set aside. Discard marinade.

2. Preheat oven to 350°.

3. Combine boiling water and grits in a bowl; stir well. Add shrimp, 2 tablespoons cheese, parsley, 1 teaspoon lemon rind, and pepper; stir well.

4. Spoon grits mixture into a 2-quart casserole coated with cooking spray; sprinkle with remaining 2 tablespoons cheese and paprika. Bake at 350° for 30 minutes. Garnish with basil sprigs, if desired. Yield: 6 servings (serving size: 1 cup).

POINTS: 4; **Exchanges:** 2 Starch, 1½ Very Lean Meat
Per serving: CAL 218 (19% from fat); PRO 16.6g; FAT 4.7g (sat 1.1g); CARB 28.2g; FIB 1.9g; CHOL 89mg; IRON 16mg; SOD 807mg; CALC 91mg

Fiery Chicken Burritos

We tested this recipe with a roasted chicken from the grocery store deli to save time. If you choose to, be sure to remove the skin.

1 cup uncooked bulgur or cracked wheat
1 tablespoon vegetable oil
8 green onions, cut into ½-inch slices
2 cups seeded chopped tomato, divided
1 cup chopped roasted chicken breast
2 tablespoons to ¼ cup chopped pickled jalapeño pepper

Bulgur consists of whole-wheat kernels that have been steamed, hulled, and cracked, resulting in reduced cooking time; the finer the grind, the less cooking time required. Bulgur has a tender, chewy texture and nutty flavor that makes it popular in salads, such as tabbouleh.

Shopping
Bulgur is available in coarse, medium, and fine grinds. Choose bulgur that smells fresh and nutty.

Storage
Keep bulgur in an airtight container in the refrigerator or freezer.

Multigrain Pancakes and fresh fruit make a hearty and satisfying breakfast.

Multigrain Pancakes

1   cup low-fat buttermilk
3   tablespoons vegetable oil
2   large egg whites, lightly beaten
1½ cups Multigrain Pancake Mix
Cooking spray

1. Combine first 3 ingredients in a bowl; stir well. Add pancake mix, and stir until smooth (batter will be slightly thick).

2. Spoon about ¼ cup batter for each pancake onto a hot nonstick griddle or skillet coated with cooking spray. Turn pancakes when tops are covered with bubbles and edges look cooked. Serve with maple syrup or honey, if desired. Yield: 10 pancakes (serving size: 1 pancake).

POINTS 3; **Exchanges:** 1 Starch, 1 Fat
Per serving: CAL 121 (36% from fat); PRO 3.7g; FAT 4.9g (sat 1.1g); CARB 16g; FIB 0.1g; CHOL 0mg; IRON 0.9mg; SOD 203mg; CALC 56mg

---

2   tablespoons white balsamic vinegar
2   tablespoons Dijon mustard
¼   teaspoon pepper
4   (10-inch) flour tortillas
1   cup (4 ounces) shredded reduced-fat sharp cheddar cheese
Cooking spray

1. Cook bulgur according to directions, omitting salt. Drain; set aside.

2. Preheat oven to 350°.

3. Heat oil in a large skillet over medium-high heat. Sauté onions until tender. Add bulgur, and cook 10 minutes, stirring constantly. Stir in 1 cup tomato, chicken, and next 4 ingredients. Divide mixture evenly among tortillas, and sprinkle with cheddar cheese. Fold over all 4 sides of each tortilla to form a pouch. Place pouches, folded sides down, in a 13- x 9-inch baking dish coated with cooking spray.

4. Cover and bake at 350° for 10 minutes or until thoroughly heated. Sprinkle remaining 1 cup tomato over burritos. Yield: 4 servings (serving size: 1 burrito and ¼ cup tomato).

POINTS: 8; **Exchanges:** 4 Starch, 2 Very Lean Meat, 2 Fat
Per serving: CAL 478 (27% from fat); PRO 25.9g; FAT 14.2g (sat 4.5g); CARB 63.8g; FIB 11.5g; CHOL 40mg; IRON 3.7mg; SOD 1,010mg; CALC 302mg

---

Multigrain Pancake Mix:

½   cup regular oats
2   cups all-purpose flour
½   cup whole-wheat flour
½   cup cornmeal
¼   cup wheat bran
¼   cup toasted wheat germ
¼   cup sugar
2   teaspoons baking powder
1½ teaspoons salt
1   teaspoon baking soda

1. Place oats in a food processor, and process until smooth. Add remaining ingredients, and process until well blended. Store in a tightly sealed container in refrigerator. Yield: 4 cups.

"Oven-Fried" Dill Pickles

½   cup yellow cornmeal
⅓   cup grated Parmesan cheese
1   teaspoon paprika
¼   teaspoon ground red pepper
1   (32-ounce) jar hamburger dill pickle slices, drained
Cooking spray

1. Preheat oven to 450°.

2. Combine first 4 ingredients in a shallow dish or pie plate; stir well.

3. Press pickle slices between paper towels until barely moist; dredge in cornmeal mixture. Place pickles on a large baking sheet coated with cooking spray. Lightly coat pickles with cooking spray. Bake at 450° for 12 minutes or until golden. Let stand 5 minutes before serving. Yield: 19 servings (serving size: 7 pickles).

POINTS: 0; **Exchanges:** Free
Per serving: CAL 19 (28% from fat); PRO 0.9g; FAT 0.6g (sat 0.3g); CARB 2.6g; FIB 0.4g; CHOL 1mg; IRON 0.2mg; SOD 417mg; CALC 20mg

Eight-Vegetable Soup With Millet

1   cup water
¼   cup uncooked millet
1   tablespoon stick margarine
3   cups coarsely chopped onion
5   (10½-ounce) cans low-salt chicken broth
2¼ cups coarsely chopped zucchini
2   cups coarsely chopped carrot
2   cups coarsely chopped red potato
2   cups coarsely chopped fresh green beans
2   cups coarsely chopped tomato
1½ cups coarsely chopped celery with leaves
1   teaspoon salt
½   teaspoon pepper
½   teaspoon dried basil
½   teaspoon dried thyme
1   bay leaf
1   cup 1% low-fat milk
1   cup thinly sliced fresh spinach

1. Bring water to a boil in a medium saucepan; add millet. Cover, reduce heat, and simmer 25 minutes or until millet is tender and liquid is absorbed. Remove from heat; fluff with a fork, and set aside.

2. Melt margarine over medium-high heat in a large Dutch oven. Add onion; sauté 5 minutes. Add broth and next 11 ingredients; bring to a boil. Reduce heat, and simmer, uncovered, 45 minutes or until vegetables are tender. Remove from heat; discard bay leaf.

3. Place 2 cups soup in a food processor or blender; process 30 seconds or until smooth. Pour into a bowl. Repeat procedure with remaining soup. Return puréed soup to pan; stir in millet, milk, and spinach. Cook over medium heat 5 minutes or until thoroughly heated. Yield: 15 servings (serving size: 1 cup).

Note: Freeze extra soup in an airtight container for up to 3 months, if desired.

POINTS: 1; **Exchanges:** 1 Starch
Per serving: CAL 93 (19% from fat); PRO 5.8g; FAT 2g (sat 0.5g); CARB 14g; FIB 2.9g; CHOL 12mg; IRON 1.1mg; SOD 230mg; CALC 55mg

Peanut Butter-and-Banana Rice Pudding

Be sure to use brown-spotted, sweet, ripe bananas for this recipe.

4   cups cooked long-grain rice
½   cup raisins
Butter-flavored cooking spray
1   medium banana, sliced
2   tablespoons orange juice
1¼   cups 2% reduced-fat milk
½   cup sugar
¼   cup creamy peanut butter
1   teaspoon vanilla extract
⅛   teaspoon salt
1   large egg

1. Combine rice and raisins; toss gently. Spoon into a 1½-quart casserole coated with cooking spray. Set aside.

MILLET

This slightly sweet grain is rich in iron, amino acids, and B vitamins. Toasting millet in a skillet prevents clumping and adds a nutty flavor.

Shopping

Millet is available at health-food stores and Asian markets.

Storage

Millet will keep for about two months in an airtight container in a cool, dark, dry place or for four months in the refrigerator and up to six months in the freezer.

Eight-Vegetable Soup With Millet

AMARANTH

A mildly spicy, nutty-flavored seed, amaranth is very high in protein. It can be cooked in liquid until creamy or stirred into bread batter raw.

Shopping

Look for amaranth at health-food stores and Caribbean and Asian markets. It is available whole, ground into flour, puffed, and processed into pasta and cereal.

Storage

Keep amaranth in an airtight container in a cool, dark, dry place (it develops a bitter taste if it's exposed to light); it will keep for up to one year. Amaranth flour should be tightly covered and stored in the freezer or refrigerator for up to six months.

2. Preheat oven to 350°.

3. Place banana slices and orange juice in a blender; process until smooth. With blender on, add milk and next 5 ingredients; process until smooth. Pour banana mixture over rice mixture. Place casserole in a baking dish; add hot water to baking dish to a depth of 1 inch. Bake, uncovered, at 350° for 1 hour or until set. Remove casserole from water bath immediately; let cool slightly. Serve warm, at room temperature, or chilled. Yield: 8 servings (serving size: ⅔ cup).

POINTS: 6; **Exchanges:** 2½ Starch, 1 Fruit, ½ Fat
Per serving: CAL 281 (19% from fat); PRO 6.9g; FAT 5.8g (sat 1.4g); CARB 51.6g; FIB 1.9g; CHOL 30mg; IRON 1.4mg; SOD 104mg; CALC 69mg

Savory Provolone Scones

1¾ cups all-purpose flour
¾ cup (3 ounces) shredded provolone cheese
½ cup uncooked whole-grain amaranth
1½ teaspoons baking powder
1 teaspoon dried Italian seasoning
¼ teaspoon salt
¼ teaspoon pepper
2 tablespoons chilled stick margarine, cut into small pieces
¾ cup skim milk
Cooking spray
1 large egg white, lightly beaten
1½ tablespoons uncooked whole-grain amaranth
¼ teaspoon salt

1. Preheat oven to 425°.

2. Combine first 7 ingredients in a bowl, and toss well. Cut in margarine with a pastry blender or 2 knives until mixture resembles coarse meal. Add milk, stirring just until moist.

3. Turn dough out onto a lightly floured surface; with floured hands, knead lightly 4 times. Roll dough to ½-inch thickness. Cut into 18 (2-inch) diamonds using a sharp knife dipped in flour.

4. Place scones 1 inch apart on baking sheets coated with cooking spray, and brush with egg white; sprinkle with 1½ tablespoons amaranth and ¼ teaspoon salt. Bake at 425° for 15 minutes

or until lightly browned. Yield: 1½ dozen (serving size: 1 scone).

POINTS: 2; **Exchanges:** 1 Starch, ½ Fat
Per serving: CAL 96 (27% from fat); PRO 3.8g; FAT 2.9g (sat 1.2g); CARB 13.2g; FIB 0.7g; CHOL 3mg; IRON 1.9mg; SOD 130mg; CALC 78mg

Couscous With Glazed Vegetables

2 cups fat-free chicken broth
1 (10-ounce) package uncooked couscous
Cooking spray
1 teaspoon olive oil
1½ cups julienne-cut carrot
1½ cups julienne-cut zucchini
⅔ cup (1-inch) sliced green onions
2 garlic cloves, minced
3 tablespoons low-salt soy sauce
3 tablespoons mango chutney
2 tablespoons chopped walnuts
1 tablespoon brown sugar
1 tablespoon water

1. Bring broth to a boil in a medium saucepan; gradually stir in couscous. Remove from heat; cover and let stand 5 minutes. Fluff with a fork.

2. Coat a large skillet with cooking spray. Add oil; place over high heat until hot. Add carrot; sauté 2 minutes. Reduce heat to medium. Add next 3 ingredients; sauté 2 minutes. Stir in soy sauce and next 4 ingredients; bring to a boil. Combine glazed vegetables and couscous, tossing gently to coat. Yield: 7 servings (serving size: 1 cup).

POINTS: 4; **Exchanges:** 2½ Starch, 2 Veg
Per serving: CAL 217 (10% from fat); PRO 8.7g; FAT 2.5g (sat 0.2g); CARB 40.9g; FIB 2.7g; CHOL 0mg; IRON 1.4mg; SOD 394mg; CALC 23mg

Grilled Tuna-and-Pearl Barley Niçoise

½ cup fresh lemon juice
1 tablespoon thinly sliced fresh basil
2 tablespoons extra-virgin olive oil
2 tablespoons anchovy paste
2 teaspoons herbes de Provence
¼ teaspoon pepper
4 garlic cloves, minced
4 cups water
1 cup uncooked pearl barley

3 cups (1-inch) sliced green beans (about ½ pound)
2 hard-cooked large eggs
1 cup finely chopped fennel bulb
½ cup thinly sliced red onion, separated into rings
2 large tomatoes, cut into ¼-inch-thick wedges (about ¾ pound)
2 tablespoons cracked pepper
6 (6-ounce) tuna steaks (about ¾ inch thick)
Cooking spray
18 niçoise olives

1. Combine first 7 ingredients in a small bowl; stir well with a whisk. Set aside.

2. Bring 4 cups water to a boil in a saucepan. Add barley; cover, reduce heat, and simmer 45 minutes or until barley is tender and liquid is absorbed. Remove from heat; let stand, covered, 5 minutes. Spoon barley into a large bowl; set aside.

3. Drop green beans into a large saucepan of boiling water; cook 2 minutes. Drain and rinse under cold water. Add beans to barley; set aside.

4. Cut eggs in half lengthwise; remove and reserve yolks. Slice egg whites. Add egg white, lemon juice mixture, fennel, onion, and tomatoes to barley mixture; toss gently. Set aside.

5. Prepare grill. Press cracked pepper into both sides of tuna steaks. Place tuna on grill rack coated with cooking spray; grill 3 minutes on each side until tuna is medium-rare or desired degree of doneness. Place 1½ cups barley mixture, 1 tuna steak, and 3 olives on each of 6 plates. Yield: 6 servings.

POINTS: 9; **Exchanges:** 2 Fat, 2 Starch, 6 Very Lean Meat, 1 Veg **Per serving:** CAL 476 (29% from fat); PRO 47.6g; FAT 15.6g (sat 3.1g); CARB 37.1g; FIB 7.7g; CHOL 65mg; IRON 4.9mg; SOD 884mg; CALC 83mg

Beef-and-Barley-Stuffed Peppers

4 medium green bell peppers
¾ pound ground round
1 cup chopped onion

Barley creates a wonderfully chewy base for Grilled Tuna-and-Pearl Barley Niçoise.

½ cup chopped celery
2 garlic cloves, minced
Cooking spray
1 cup cooked pearl barley
1 cup fresh corn kernels (about 2 ears) or frozen whole-kernel corn, thawed
2 teaspoons chili powder
½ teaspoon salt
½ teaspoon dried oregano
1½ teaspoons 72%-less-salt Worcestershire sauce
⅛ teaspoon pepper
1 (8-ounce) can no-salt-added tomato sauce
1 cup (4 ounces) shredded reduced-fat sharp cheddar cheese, divided

1. Cut tops off peppers; discard tops, seeds, and membranes. Drop peppers in boiling water, and cook 4 minutes; drain and set aside.

2. Cook beef and next 3 ingredients in a large skillet coated with cooking spray over medium-high heat until browned, stirring to crumble beef. Drain in a colander; return to skillet.

3. Preheat oven to 350°.

4. Add barley and next 7 ingredients to beef mixture; stir well. Stir in ½ cup cheese. Spoon 1 cup beef mixture into each bell pepper. Place stuffed peppers in an 8-inch square baking dish. Bake at 350° for 15 minutes. Sprinkle remaining ½ cup

Give your diet a boost of fiber with Beef-and-Barley-Stuffed Peppers.

cheese evenly over peppers; bake an additional 5 minutes or until cheese melts. Yield: 4 servings (serving size: 1 stuffed pepper).

POINTS: 7; **Exchanges:** 1 Veg, 2 Starch, 1 Med-fat Meat, 2 Lean Meat
Per serving: CAL 364 (29% from fat); PRO 31.3g; FAT 11.7g (sat 5.2g); CARB 36g; FIB 6.2g; CHOL 71mg; IRON 3.9mg; SOD 634mg; CALC 291mg

Roasted Shallot-and-Swiss Cheese Pie

For a meatless entrée, you can simply omit the country ham.

2 cups water
1 cup uncooked seven whole grains and sesame breakfast pilaf (such as Kashi)
15 shallots (about ¾ pound)
Cooking spray
1 tablespoon olive oil
½ cup minced lean country ham (about 3 ounces)
1 tablespoon cornstarch
1 cup 1% low-fat milk
2 tablespoons dry white wine
¼ teaspoon salt
¼ teaspoon pepper
⅛ teaspoon garlic powder
1 large egg
1 (7-ounce) can refrigerated breadstick dough
½ cup (2 ounces) shredded reduced-fat Swiss cheese

1. Preheat oven to 375°.

2. Bring water to a boil in a medium saucepan, and stir in pilaf. Cover saucepan, reduce heat to medium, and cook 25 minutes or until liquid is absorbed. Set aside.

3. Place shallots on a jelly-roll pan coated with cooking spray. Drizzle oil over shallots; toss to coat. Bake at 375° for 45 minutes. Add pilaf mixture and ham. Bake an additional 15 minutes or until pilaf mixture is toasted. Remove from oven; set aside. Reduce oven temperature to 350°.

4. Combine cornstarch and milk in a small bowl; stir with a whisk until blended. Add wine and next 4 ingredients; stir well, and set aside.

5. Unroll breadstick dough, separating into strips.

Working on a flat surface, coil 1 strip of dough around itself in a spiral pattern. Add second strip of dough to end of first; pinch ends together to seal. Continue coiling dough. Repeat with remaining strips. Roll dough into a 13-inch circle; fit into a 9-inch quiche dish coated with cooking spray.

6. Sprinkle cheese into bottom of prepared crust; top with shallot mixture. Pour egg mixture over shallot mixture. Bake at 350° for 45 minutes or until set. Let stand 10 minutes before serving. Yield: 8 servings.

Note: A sharp serrated knife works best for cutting this pie.

POINTS: 5; **Exchanges:** 2 Starch, 1 Med-fat Meat
Per serving: CAL 230 (30% from fat); PRO 10.7g; FAT 7.6g (sat 2.1g); CARB 29.3g; FIB 2.2g; CHOL 42mg; IRON 1.9mg; SOD 518mg; CALC 128mg

Beef-and-Creamed Spinach Whole Grain Casserole

1   (10-ounce) package frozen chopped spinach, thawed
4   ounces block-style fat-free cream cheese, cubed and softened
1   tablespoon fresh lemon juice
1   tablespoon stick margarine
1   cup water
1   cup fat-free beef broth
1   cup uncooked seven whole grains and sesame breakfast pilaf (such as Kashi)
Cooking spray
½   pound ground round
1   cup chopped onion
1   cup grated carrot
¼   cup minced celery
2   garlic cloves, minced
1   teaspoon dried basil
½   teaspoon dried oregano
½   teaspoon salt
½   teaspoon pepper
2   tablespoons grated Parmesan cheese

1. Cook spinach according to microwave directions on package using a 1-quart microwave-safe baking dish; drain well, and return to dish. Immediately add cream cheese, lemon juice, and margarine to hot spinach, stirring until cheese and margarine melt. Set aside.

2. Bring water and broth to a boil in a medium saucepan. Stir in pilaf; cover, reduce heat to medium, and simmer 25 minutes or until liquid is absorbed. Set aside.

3. Preheat oven to 350°.

4. Coat a large skillet with cooking spray, and place over medium-high heat until hot. Add ground round, onion, carrot, celery, and garlic; cook until ground round is browned and vegetables are tender, stirring to crumble. Drain well, and return beef mixture to pan. Stir in basil, oregano, salt, and pepper. Add cooked pilaf, and toss well.

5. Spread half of ground round mixture into bottom of a 1½-quart baking dish coated with cooking spray. Top with spinach mixture, spreading to edges of dish. Spread remaining ground round mixture evenly over spinach mixture; sprinkle with Parmesan cheese. Cover and bake at 350° for 30 minutes; uncover and bake an additional 10 minutes. Let stand 15 minutes before serving. Yield: 6 servings (serving size: 1 cup).

POINTS: 3; **Exchanges:** 1 Starch, 1 Veg, 1½ Lean Meat
Per serving: CAL 187 (29% from fat); PRO 15.9g; FAT 6g (sat 1.6g); CARB 17.4g; FIB 4.4g; CHOL 28mg; IRON 2.3mg; SOD 433mg; CALC 143mg

Chocolate-Drizzled Pretzel Rods

⅓   cup honey crunch wheat germ
1   large egg white, lightly beaten
15   pretzel rods (about 5 ounces)
Cooking spray
½   cup semisweet chocolate chips, melted

1. Preheat oven to 350°.

2. Place wheat germ in a shallow dish or pie plate. Brush egg white evenly over pretzels; dredge in wheat germ. Place on a large baking sheet coated with cooking spray. Bake at 350° for 10 minutes. Drizzle with melted chocolate, and let cool completely. Yield: 15 servings (serving size: 1 pretzel).

POINTS: 2; **Exchanges:** 1 Starch
Per serving: CAL 78 (30% from fat); PRO 2.3g; FAT 2.6g (sat 1.1g); CARB 12.3g; FIB 0.6g; CHOL 0mg; IRON 0.7mg; SOD 207mg; CALC 2mg

WHEAT GERM

Wheat germ, the seed of the wheat kernel, is rich in vitamins, minerals, and protein. This grain is widely available and has an aromatic, nutty taste. It is most often used to add nutrients to recipes.

Shopping

Wheat germ is available in two flavors: toasted and honey crunch. Look for it on the cereal aisle of health-food stores and most supermarkets.

Storage

Always store wheat germ in the refrigerator, tightly covered.

Power Veggies

Breaking out of your vegetable rut may be
the key to a longer, healthier life.

Wben it comes to vegetables, Americans like to play it safe. Our five most popular vegetables are, in order, potatoes, iceberg lettuce, tomatoes, onions, and carrots. Sounds harmless enough—until you consider that 40% of the vegetables Americans eat come in the form of French fries and mashed potatoes. And iceberg lettuce is hardly considered a power veggie. It's not just a cliche: Variety is indeed the spice of life, especially when it comes to your diet. Think of it as nutritional cross-training—diets that include a wide variety of foods not only enhance the body's ability to reap nutritional benefits, but may also help prevent disease. By eating a varied diet, you increase the amount of vitamins, minerals, fiber, and phytochemicals (chemicals found in certain foods that appear to fight cancer) that your body consumes. Variety may also help you live longer: A 1993 study found that people who ate the widest variety of foods had a lower risk of dying prematurely than those who stuck to the same series of recipes night after night. Make a point of using these recipes to try a new vegetable at least once a week. After tasting Kale-and-Spinach Bake and Chilled Beet-and-Fennel Soup, you'll never go back to iceberg lettuce.

Beef and Broccoli With Oyster Sauce will make Chinese take-out a thing of the past.

The boxed mix used to make Vidalia Onion Pizza lends homemade flavor without the fuss.

Beef and Broccoli With Oyster Sauce

3   tablespoons oyster sauce
1   tablespoon low-salt soy sauce
1   tablespoon dry sherry
1   tablespoon water
2   teaspoons sugar
1   teaspoon cornstarch
1   pound lean flank steak
1   tablespoon cornstarch
2   tablespoons water
1   tablespoon low-salt soy sauce
2   teaspoons sugar
1   tablespoon vegetable oil, divided
⅓   cup (½-inch) diagonally sliced green onions
1   tablespoon peeled minced fresh ginger
6   cups fresh broccoli florets (about 1 pound)
¼   cup water
6   cups hot cooked long-grain rice

1. Combine first 6 ingredients; set aside.

2. Trim fat from steak. Cut diagonally across grain into thin slices. Combine 1 tablespoon cornstarch and next 3 ingredients. Add steak; cover and marinate in refrigerator 15 minutes.

3. Heat 2 teaspoons oil in a nonstick skillet over high heat. Add steak mixture; stir-fry 2 minutes. Remove steak from pan; set aside. Add remaining 1 teaspoon oil, onions, and ginger; stir-fry over medium-high heat 30 seconds. Stir in broccoli and ¼ cup water; cover and cook 3 minutes. Return steak to pan, and stir in sauce mixture; stir-fry 2 minutes. Serve with rice. Yield: 6 servings (serving size: 1 cup beef mixture and 1 cup rice).

POINTS: 9; **Exchanges:** 3½ Starch, 1 Veg, 1½ Lean Meat, 1 Fat
Per serving: CAL 424 (21% from fat); PRO 22.2g; FAT 9.9g (sat 3.5g); CARB 60.4g; FIB 3.9g; CHOL 38mg; IRON 4.4mg; SOD 505mg; CALC 73mg

KOHLRABI

Vidalia Onion Pizza

1   (16-ounce) box hot roll mix
1⅓ cups very warm water (120° to 130°)
¼   cup all-purpose flour
Cooking spray
2½ teaspoons olive oil, divided
6   cups slivered Vidalia or other sweet onion
      (about 1½ pounds)
1½ cups (6 ounces) shredded Jarlsberg or
      Swiss cheese
½   cup (2 ounces) shredded Asiago or
      Parmesan cheese

1. Combine hot roll mix and enclosed yeast
packet in a large bowl, and stir well. Add 1⅓
cups very warm water, and stir well. Turn dough
out onto a lightly floured surface. Knead until
smooth and elastic (about 5 minutes); add ¼ cup
flour, 1 tablespoon at a time, as needed, to prevent dough from sticking to hands. Cover dough,
and let rest 5 minutes. Divide dough in half. Roll
each half of dough into a 12-inch circle on a
lightly floured surface. Place on 2 (12-inch) pizza
pans or baking sheets coated with cooking spray;
pierce dough several times with a fork. Cover and
let rise in a warm place (85°), free from drafts, 15
minutes or until puffy. Brush ½ teaspoon olive
oil over each crust.

2. Preheat oven to 450°.

3. Heat remaining 1½ teaspoons olive oil in a
large Dutch oven over medium heat. Add Vidalia
onion, and sauté 20 minutes or until onion is
golden brown.

4. Sprinkle ¾ cup shredded Jarlsberg cheese over
each pizza crust. Divide caramelized onion evenly
between each pizza; sprinkle each with ¼ cup
shredded Asiago cheese. Bake pizzas at 450° for
15 minutes or until lightly browned. Cut each
pizza into 8 wedges. Yield: 8 servings (serving
size: 2 wedges).

Note: You can sauté the onions while the pizza
crusts rise.

POINTS: 8; **Exchanges:** 3 Starch, 1 Med-fat Meat, 1 Veg, ½ Fat
Per serving: CAL 381 (29% from fat); PRO 15.9g; FAT 12.3g (sat
6g); CARB 49.9g; FIB 3.6g; CHOL 28mg; IRON 3mg; SOD 563mg;
CALC 317mg

Turkey-Vegetable Stew

½   cup all-purpose flour, divided
1½ pounds turkey tenderloin, cut into 1-inch
      pieces
Cooking spray
1   tablespoon vegetable oil
½   cup chopped onion
2   cups peeled cubed kohlrabi (about
      1 pound)
1½ cups coarsely chopped green cabbage
1   cup sliced carrot
6   small red potatoes (about ¾ pound),
      peeled and quartered
½   to 1 teaspoon dried thyme
½   teaspoon dried sage
2   (14¼-ounce) cans fat-free chicken broth
2   cups small fresh broccoli florets
2   (14.5-ounce) cans no-salt-added whole
      tomatoes, drained and coarsely chopped
½   cup water
1   teaspoon salt
¼   teaspoon pepper

1. Combine ¼ cup flour and turkey in a large
zip-top plastic bag; seal bag, and shake to coat
turkey with flour.

2. Coat a large Dutch oven with cooking spray;
add vegetable oil, and place over medium-high
heat until hot. Add turkey pieces and chopped
onion, and cook 6 minutes or until turkey loses
its pink color. Add cubed kohlrabi and next 6
ingredients; bring mixture to a boil. Cover,
reduce heat, and simmer 20 minutes or until
potatoes are tender. Add broccoli florets
and tomatoes, and cook, uncovered, 5
minutes or until broccoli is tender.

3. Place remaining ¼ cup flour in a
medium bowl, and gradually add ½
cup water, stirring with a whisk until well
blended. Add flour to stew, and stir in salt and
pepper, and cook over medium heat for 5 minutes or until stew is thick, stirring frequently.
Yield: 6 servings (serving size: 1½ cups).

POINTS: 6; **Exchanges:** 1½ Starch, 3½ Very Lean Meat, ½ Fat,
1 Veg
Per serving: CAL 293 (17% from fat); PRO 30.4g; FAT 5.5g (sat
1.4g); CARB 29.1g; FIB 3.7g; CHOL 59mg; IRON 3.3mg; SOD
489mg; CALC 98mg

A member of the
turnip family,
kohlrabi tastes like
a mild, sweet turnip
and is rich in potassium
and vitamin C. Although
it's best steamed,
kohlrabi can also be
stir-fried or added to
soups and stews.

Shopping
Kohlrabi should be
heavy for its size and
have richly colored
green leaves. Avoid
bulbs with turning leaf
tips or soft spots. For
tender kohlrabi, choose
bulbs no bigger than
3 inches in diameter.

Storage
Refrigerate kohlrabi,
tightly wrapped, for up
to four days.

ARTICHOKES

Artichokes are a low-calorie (there are only 25 calories in a whole artichoke), low-sodium food. They are a good source of fiber, vitamin C, magnesium, and folate.

Shopping

Look for deep-green artichokes that are heavy for their size and have tight leaves. Small artichokes are more tender than larger ones.

Storage

Store artichokes in a securely sealed plastic bag in the refrigerator for up to four days.

Greek Lamb-and-Artichoke Soup

Part of the broth is combined with the eggs before they are added to the soup. This technique, which is known as tempering, prevents the eggs from curdling.

```
10   cups water
3    medium leeks, trimmed and cut in half
2    bay leaves
1    medium onion, peeled and cut in half
1    fennel bulb, trimmed and quartered
1½   pounds lean ground lamb
1    cup fresh breadcrumbs
½    cup tomato juice
2    teaspoons dried dill
½    teaspoon salt
½    teaspoon dried oregano
½    teaspoon pepper
2    garlic cloves, minced
2    cups hot cooked long-grain rice
⅓    cup fresh lemon juice
2    (15-ounce) cans cannellini beans or other
     white beans, drained
2    (14-ounce) cans quartered artichoke
     hearts, drained
2    large eggs
```

1. Combine first 5 ingredients in a large Dutch oven; bring to a boil. Partially cover, reduce heat, and simmer 45 minutes. Remove from heat, and set stock aside.

2. Combine lamb and next 7 ingredients in a bowl; stir well. Shape mixture into 24 (1¼-inch) meatballs. Place a large nonstick skillet over medium-high heat until hot. Add meatballs; cook 10 minutes, browning on all sides. Remove from skillet; drain meatballs on paper towels.

3. Strain stock through a colander into a large bowl; discard solids. Reserve 2 cups stock; set aside. Return remaining stock to pan, and bring to a boil; add meatballs, rice, and next 3 ingredients. Return to a boil, and reduce heat to low.

4. Place eggs in a bowl; stir well. Gradually add reserved 2 cups stock, stirring constantly with a whisk. Slowly drizzle egg mixture into soup, stirring constantly. Remove from heat; serve immediately. Yield: 7 servings (serving size: 2 cups).

Note: Reheat the soup over medium-low heat. If the soup is allowed to boil, the eggs will curdle.

POINTS: 8; **Exchanges:** 3½ Lean Meat, 2½ Starch, 1 Veg
Per serving: CAL 404 (20% from fat); PRO 34.1g; FAT 9.2g (sat 3.2g); CARB 46.4g; FIB 3.4g; CHOL 130mg; IRON 5.3mg; SOD 774mg; CALC 109mg

Sesame Broccoli and Carrots

```
5    cups fresh broccoli florets
1    cup julienne-cut carrot
1    teaspoon cornstarch
¼    cup low-salt chicken broth
1½   tablespoons low-salt soy sauce
1½   tablespoons dry sherry
1    teaspoon vegetable oil
1    tablespoon peeled minced fresh ginger
2    garlic cloves, minced
½    teaspoon dark sesame oil
1    teaspoon sesame seeds, toasted
```

STEP BY STEP: COOKING ARTICHOKES

Wash artichokes. Cut off stem end so artichoke sits upright.

Remove bottom leaves.

Trim ½ inch from top of artichoke. Rub edges with lemon. Cook according to preferred method.

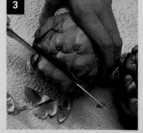

After cooking, pull off outer leaves; reserve for use. Thin inner leaves, choke, and bottom will remain.

Remove thin inner leaves; remove thistle center from bottom with spoon.

Sesame Broccoli and Carrots
with Gingered Flounder
(page 79) and Almond Rice
Pilaf (page 79)

Brussels Sprouts-and-Broccoli Frittata is a hearty brunch entrée with less than 150 calories.

1. Bring 8 cups water to a boil in a Dutch oven. Add broccoli and carrot; cover and cook 3 minutes. Drain and rinse under cold water; drain well.

2. Combine cornstarch and next 3 ingredients in a small bowl; stir well, and set aside.

3. Heat vegetable oil in a large nonstick skillet or wok over medium-high heat. Add ginger and garlic, and stir-fry 10 seconds. Add broccoli and carrot, and stir-fry 1 minute. Add chicken broth mixture, and bring to a boil. Cook 1 minute or until mixture is thick, stirring constantly. Remove from heat; stir in sesame oil, and sprinkle with toasted sesame seeds. Yield: 4 servings (serving size: 1 cup).

POINTS: 1; **Exchanges:** 2 Veg, ½ Fat
Per serving: CAL 73 (32% from fat); PRO 4g; FAT 2.6g (sat 0.4g); CARB 10.4g; FIB 4.4g; CHOL 0mg; IRON 1.3mg; SOD 191mg; CALC 71mg

Brussels Sprouts-and-Broccoli Frittata

Cooking spray
½ cup chopped onion
1   cup small fresh broccoli florets
1   cup thinly sliced Brussels sprouts
½ cup diced turkey ham
1   garlic clove, minced
⅓ cup cooked vermicelli or spaghetti (about ½ ounce uncooked)
¼ cup (1 ounce) grated fresh Parmesan cheese, divided
2   large eggs, lightly beaten
4   large egg whites, lightly beaten
¼ teaspoon crushed red pepper

1. Coat a nonstick skillet with cooking spray; place over medium heat until hot. Add onion; sauté 3 minutes. Add broccoli and next 3 ingredients; sauté 2 minutes. Spoon mixture into a bowl. Stir

BRUSSELS SPROUTS

in pasta, 2 tablespoons cheese, eggs, and egg whites.

2. Recoat skillet with cooking spray; place over medium heat until hot. Pour egg mixture into skillet. Cover, reduce heat to medium-low, and cook 8 minutes or until almost set. Sprinkle with remaining 2 tablespoons cheese and pepper. Wrap handle of skillet with foil; broil 1 minute. Cut into wedges; serve warm. Yield: 4 servings (serving size: 1 wedge).

POINTS: 3; **Exchanges:** 1 Veg, 1½ Lean Meat, ½ Starch
Per serving: CAL 147 (36% from fat); PRO 14g; FAT 5.9g (sat 2.3g); CARB 9.7g; FIB 2.3g; CHOL 115mg; IRON 1.3mg; SOD 422mg; CALC 126mg

Southwestern Carrot Slaw

A food processor with a shredding blade makes quick work of shredding the carrot and jicama.

3 cups peeled shredded carrot (about 1 pound)
1½ cups peeled shredded jicama (about ½ pound)
¾ cup chopped red bell pepper
½ cup chopped fresh cilantro
¼ cup fresh lime juice
2 tablespoons water
2 teaspoons ground cumin
2 teaspoons olive oil
½ teaspoon chili powder
¼ teaspoon salt

1. Combine first 4 ingredients in a medium bowl. Combine lime juice and next 5 ingredients;

stir well with a whisk. Pour juice mixture over slaw; toss well. Cover and chill. Stir well before serving. Yield: 5 servings (serving size: 1 cup).

POINTS: 1; **Exchanges:** 2 Veg, ½ Fat
Per serving: CAL 73 (28% from fat); PRO 1.5g; FAT 2.3g (sat 0.3g); CARB 13g; FIB 3.6g; CHOL 0mg; IRON 1.8mg; SOD 150mg; CALC 41mg

Creamy Turnip Soup
With Greens

The hot pepper sauce that contains whole peppers packed in vinegar makes a perfect condiment for this soup. It's a takeoff on Southern-style greens with pepper sauce.

5 cups peeled diced turnip (about 2 pounds)
1½ cups water
1½ teaspoons sugar
1 teaspoon margarine
½ teaspoon salt
¾ pound fresh turnip greens
¼ teaspoon sugar
2 (10½-ounce) cans low-salt chicken broth
3 tablespoons uncooked farina or cream of wheat
1 cup 2% reduced-fat milk
1 tablespoon lemon juice
Hot pepper sauce (optional)

1. Combine first 5 ingredients in a Dutch oven. Bring to a boil; cover, reduce heat, and simmer 20 minutes or until turnip is tender. Uncover and cook over high heat 10 minutes or until excess liquid evaporates; set aside.

Brussels sprouts have been linked to lower rates of cancer. They are also rich in folic acid, iron, and antioxidants.

Shopping
Choose brightly colored sprouts that have compact heads.

Storage
Store unwashed sprouts in the refrigerator in an airtight plastic bag for up to three days. If stored any longer, sprouts develop a pungent, unpleasantly strong flavor.

COOKING BRUSSELS SPROUTS

• Try to buy Brussels sprouts that are roughly the same size so they'll all cook the same length of time. One pound yields about 4 cups.

• Before cooking Brussels sprouts, wash and blot them dry. To help sprouts cook more quickly and evenly, cut a thin slice from the stem end and cut an "X" into each stem; this allows heat to penetrate the center of the sprout more easily.

2. Remove stems from turnip greens; wash leaves thoroughly, and place in a large skillet (do not dry leaves). Place skillet over medium heat, and cook until turnip greens wilt. Remove from heat; sprinkle with ¼ teaspoon sugar, and toss well.

3. Place half of turnip greens and half of turnip mixture in a food processor or blender; process 30 seconds or until smooth. Pour into a bowl. Repeat procedure with remaining turnip greens and turnip mixture. Return puréed soup to pan; stir in chicken broth, and cook until thoroughly heated. Add farina; cook 2 minutes or until thick, stirring constantly. Stir in milk and lemon juice; cook until thoroughly heated. Serve soup with hot pepper sauce, if desired. Yield: 6 servings (serving size: 1 cup).

POINTS: 2; **Exchanges:** 1 Veg, 1 Starch
Per serving: CAL 103 (20% from fat); PRO 4.3g; FAT 2.3g (sat 0.8g); CARB 17.2g; FIB 2.8g; CHOL 3mg; IRON 1.2mg; SOD 340mg; CALC 143mg

Peppered Turkey-Watercress Burgers are a welcome change from typical backyard fare.

Peppered Turkey-Watercress Burgers

1   pound ground turkey breast
1½ cups chopped trimmed watercress
¼   cup plain low-fat yogurt
1   teaspoon cracked pepper
½   teaspoon salt
1   teaspoon cracked pepper
Cooking spray
½   cup plain low-fat yogurt
4   (1½-ounce) hamburger buns, split and toasted
1   cup trimmed watercress
4   (¼-inch-thick) slices tomato

1. Combine first 5 ingredients in a bowl; stir well. Divide mixture into 4 equal portions, shaping each into a ½-inch-thick patty. Sprinkle 1 teaspoon pepper evenly over both sides of patties, pressing pepper into burgers.

2. Prepare grill. Place patties on grill rack coated with cooking spray; grill 5 minutes on each side.

3. Spread ½ cup yogurt over cut sides of buns. Arrange ¼ cup watercress over bottom half of each bun; top each with a tomato slice, a patty, and top half of bun. Yield: 4 servings.

POINTS: 6; **Exchanges:** 3½ Very Lean Meat, 2 Starch
Per serving: CAL 295 (16% from fat); PRO 31.9g; FAT 5.2g (sat 1.2g); CARB 28.4; FIB 1g; CHOL 87mg; IRON 2.6mg; SOD 496mg; CALC 139mg

Thai Cabbage

Fish sauce and chili paste with garlic are available in Oriental markets and on the ethnic aisle of many large supermarkets.

¼ cup fresh lime juice
2 tablespoons fish sauce
2 tablespoons chili paste with garlic
1 teaspoon sugar
1 teaspoon peanut oil
1 teaspoon peeled minced fresh ginger
2 garlic cloves, minced
2 (10-ounce) bags very thinly sliced green cabbage
2 cups red bell pepper strips
1⅓ cups peeled shredded carrot
¼ cup chopped fresh cilantro

1. Combine first 4 ingredients in a bowl; stir well, and set aside.

2. Heat peanut oil in a wok or very large nonstick skillet over medium-high heat. Add ginger and garlic; sauté 1 minute. Add cabbage, bell pepper, and carrot; sauté 2 minutes. Add lime juice mixture; sauté an additional 2½ minutes or until cabbage is tender. Remove from heat, and sprinkle with chopped cilantro. Yield: 7 servings (serving size: 1 cup).

POINTS: 1; **Exchanges:** 2 Veg
Per serving: CAL 52 (14% from fat); PRO 1.9g; FAT 0.8g (sat 0.1g); CARB 10.7g; FIB 2.7g; CHOL 0mg; IRON 0.4mg; SOD 279mg; CALC 46mg

Sunflower Asparagus Salad

If white balsamic vinegar is not available in your grocery store, you may substitute regular balsamic vinegar, which gets its dark color and pungent sweetness from aging in barrels.

2 tablespoons minced shallots (about 2 shallots)
⅓ cup white balsamic vinegar
1 tablespoon water

1 teaspoon sugar
1 teaspoon stone-ground mustard
1 teaspoon olive oil
¼ teaspoon salt
⅛ teaspoon freshly ground pepper
1 pound fresh asparagus spears
1 medium yellow bell pepper
4 curly leaf lettuce leaves
2 teaspoons dry-roasted sunflower seeds

1. Combine first 8 ingredients in a large shallow dish. Add asparagus; toss gently to coat. Let stand at room temperature 30 minutes.

2. Cut yellow bell pepper in half lengthwise, and discard seeds and membranes. Place bell pepper halves, skin side up, on a foil-lined baking sheet, and flatten with palm of hand. Broil 15 minutes or until pepper is blackened and charred. Place in a heavy-duty zip-top plastic bag; seal bag, and let stand 5 minutes. Peel pepper, and cut into strips; set aside.

3. Remove asparagus spears from dish, reserving marinade.

4. Prepare grill. Place asparagus spears on grill rack, and grill 4 minutes or until crisp-tender, turning occasionally.

5. Divide asparagus and bell pepper strips evenly among lettuce-lined salad plates. Drizzle evenly with reserved marinade, and sprinkle with sunflower seeds. Yield: 4 servings.

POINTS: 1; **Exchanges:** 2 Veg, ½ Fat
Per serving: CAL 66 (34% from fat); PRO 3.9g; FAT 2.5g (sat 0.3g); CARB 9.4g; FIB 1.9g; CHOL 0mg; IRON 1.4mg; SOD 179mg; CALC 33mg

Chilled Beet-and-Fennel Soup

Fennel gives a delicate hint of licoricelike sweetness to this soup.

1 pound small fresh beets
2 teaspoons fennel seeds
¼ cup water
1 tablespoon olive oil
1¾ cups chopped fennel bulb
1 cup chopped onion
1½ cups low-fat buttermilk
½ teaspoon salt
¼ teaspoon pepper

FENNEL

Rich in vitamin A, fennel also contains a fair amount of calcium, phosphorus, and potassium.

Shopping

Look for crisp bulbs completely free of browning. Two small fennel bulbs equal about 1 pound.

Storage

Wrap fennel bulbs tightly in plastic and store them in the refrigerator for up to five days.

1. Leave root and 1 inch of stem on beets, and scrub with a brush. Place beets and fennel seeds in a saucepan, and cover with water; bring to a boil. Cover, reduce heat, and simmer 35 minutes or until tender.

2. Drain beets through a fine sieve over a bowl, reserving fennel seeds and 3 cups cooking liquid. Rinse beets under cold water, and drain. Peel beets, and cut into ½-inch cubes, reserving ¾ cup for garnish. Combine remaining beets, reserved fennel seeds, and 3 cups cooking liquid in a bowl, and set aside.

3. Combine ¼ cup water and oil in a medium nonstick skillet; place over medium-high heat until hot. Add fennel bulb and onion; bring to a boil. Cover, reduce heat, and simmer 20 minutes or until tender.

4. Combine fennel bulb mixture, beet mixture, buttermilk, salt, and pepper in a food processor or blender, and process until smooth. Pour soup into a large bowl; cover and chill thoroughly. Ladle ¾ cup soup into individual bowls, and top each with 2 tablespoons reserved beets. Yield: 6 servings.

POINTS: 2; **Exchanges:** ½ Fat, 1 Starch
Per serving: CAL 103 (31% from fat); PRO 4.6g; FAT 3.6g (sat 1g); CARB 14.4g; FIB 1.4g; CHOL 0mg; IRON 1.5mg; SOD 289mg; CALC 128mg

Sweet Potato Cake

If you love fudgy brownies and the doughy bottom crust of cobblers, you'll love this super-moist cake.

2¾ pounds medium sweet potatoes
1½ cups sugar
½ cup stick margarine, softened
2 large eggs
1 large egg white
3 cups all-purpose flour
2 teaspoons baking powder
1 teaspoon ground ginger
2 teaspoons ground cinnamon
½ teaspoon salt
Cooking spray
1 tablespoon powdered sugar

1. Preheat oven to 400°.

2. Bake sweet potatoes at 400° for 50 minutes or until tender, and let cool. Peel sweet potatoes, and mash pulp to measure 2½ cups. Set pulp aside, and reserve any remaining mashed sweet potato for another use. Reduce oven temperature to 350°.

3. Combine sugar and margarine in a large bowl; beat at medium speed of a mixer until well blended (about 5 minutes). Add eggs and egg white, 1 at a time, beating well after each addition. Add mashed sweet potato; beat well.

4. Combine flour, baking powder, ginger, cinnamon, and salt; stir well. Gradually add flour

---

STEP BY STEP: SLICING FENNEL

1. Rinse the fennel thoroughly, and trim away the base of the bulb. Next, trim the stalks from the bulb, and discard the hard outside stalks.

2. Finally, cut the bulb in half lengthwise, then crosswise into thin slices.

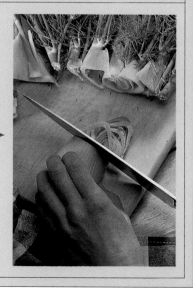

RUTABAGA

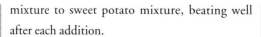

Amember of the cabbage family, this root vegetable is thought to be a cross between cabbage and turnip. And although rutabagas resemble turnips, they're larger, rounder, denser, and sweeter, but you can prepare them as you would turnips. Rutabagas contain vitamins A and C.

Shopping

Select firm rutabagas that are heavy for their size.

Storage

Store rutabagas in the refrigerator in an unsealed plastic bag for up to two weeks.

---

mixture to sweet potato mixture, beating well after each addition.

5. Pour batter into a 13- x 9-inch baking pan coated with cooking spray. Bake at 350° for 35 minutes. Let cool completely in pan on a wire rack. Sift powdered sugar evenly over cooled cake. Yield: 16 servings.

POINTS: 5; **Exchanges:** 3 Starch, ½ Fat
Per serving: CAL 257 (23% from fat); PRO 3.9g; FAT 6.7g (sat 1.4g); CARB 45.7g; FIB 1.8g; CHOL 27mg; IRON 1.5mg; SOD 157mg; CALC 43mg

Rutabaga-Carrot Pancakes

Like potato cakes, which are always an excellent side dish, these pancakes make a nice accompaniment to roast pork and veal.

3   cups peeled shredded rutabaga (about 1 pound)
1¼ cups peeled shredded carrot
⅓   cup all-purpose flour
¼   cup skim milk
½   teaspoon salt
½   teaspoon pepper
1   large egg, lightly beaten
1   large egg white, lightly beaten
Cooking spray
¼   cup low-fat sour cream
1   teaspoon prepared horseradish

1. Combine shredded rutabaga, shredded carrot, flour, skim milk, salt, pepper, egg, and egg white in a large bowl; stir well.

2. Preheat a nonstick griddle or nonstick skillet coated with cooking spray. Spoon about ¼ cup rutabaga mixture for each pancake onto hot griddle or skillet. Spread mixture to form a thin pancake, and cook 2 minutes on each side or until lightly browned. Set pancakes aside, and keep warm.

3. Combine low-fat sour cream and prepared horseradish in a small bowl, and stir well. Serve horseradish sauce with warm pancakes. Yield: 6 servings (serving size: 2 pancakes and 2 teaspoons sauce).

POINTS: 2; **Exchanges:** ½ Starch, 1 Veg, ½ Fat
Per serving: CAL 94 (23% from fat); PRO 4.1g; FAT 2.4g (sat 1.1g); CARB 14.6g; FIB 1.8g; CHOL 39mg; IRON 1mg; SOD 248mg; CALC 71mg

Creamed Celery With Blue Cheese

Because a small amount of blue cheese provides big flavor in this side dish, a ½-cup serving is very satisfying.

½   cup fat-free chicken broth
3   cups julienne-cut celery
2   tablespoons tub-style light cream cheese
⅓   cup evaporated skim milk
1   tablespoon crumbled blue cheese
2   teaspoons slivered almonds, toasted

1. Bring chicken broth to a boil in a large skillet over medium heat. Add celery, and sauté 5 minutes or until tender. Add cream cheese, stirring until cheese melts. Add milk and blue cheese, stirring until well blended. Sprinkle with slivered almonds. Serve immediately. Yield: 4 servings (serving size: ½ cup).

POINTS: 1; **Exchanges:** 2 Veg, ½ Fat
Per serving: CAL 61 (35% from fat); PRO 4g; FAT 2.4g (sat 1.2g); CARB 6.5g; FIB 1.6g; CHOL 6mg; IRON 0.5mg; SOD 227mg; CALC 119mg

Curried Cauliflower

¾   cup fat-free chicken broth
1½ teaspoons curry powder
1   teaspoon peeled minced fresh ginger
½   teaspoon ground coriander
½   teaspoon ground cumin
½   teaspoon salt
1   teaspoon olive oil
1   medium onion, quartered and sliced
6   cups cauliflower florets (about 1 medium head)

1. Combine first 6 ingredients; stir well, and set broth mixture aside.

2. Heat olive oil in a large nonstick skillet over medium heat. Add onion, and sauté 2 minutes. Stir in broth mixture and cauliflower florets. Cover and cook 8 minutes or until cauliflower is tender, stirring occasionally. Yield: 5 servings (serving size: 1 cup).

POINTS: 1; **Exchanges:** 2 Veg, ½ Fat
Per serving: CAL 70 (18% from fat); PRO 3.8g; FAT 1.4g (sat 0.5g); CARB 12.8g; FIB 4.4g; CHOL 0mg; IRON 1mg; SOD 345mg; CALC 46mg

Green Pea Guacamole

1   (10-ounce) package frozen green peas
1   cup peeled cubed avocado
½   cup fat-free sour cream
¼   cup chopped green onions
2   tablespoons chopped fresh cilantro
1½ tablespoons fresh lime juice
1   tablespoon drained canned chopped green
     chiles
¼   teaspoon salt
⅛   teaspoon pepper
1   garlic clove, peeled

1. Cook peas according to package directions, and drain. Place peas and remaining ingredients in a food processor, and process until smooth. Spoon guacamole into a bowl; cover and chill. Serve with baked tortilla chips Yield: 9 servings (serving size: ¼ cup).

POINTS: 1; **Exchanges:** ½ Starch, ½ Fat
Per serving: CAL 63 (39% from fat); PRO 3g; FAT 2.7g (sat 0.4g); CARB 7.1g; FIB 1.9g; CHOL 0mg; IRON 0.8mg; SOD 112mg; CALC 26mg

Fresh Tomato Pasta Pie

We found that this recipe works best when the pasta is broken in half before boiling.

3½ cups cooked angel hair (about 5 ounces
     uncooked pasta)
½   cup chopped fresh basil, divided
¼   teaspoon salt
¼   teaspoon pepper
2   large eggs, lightly beaten
4   large egg whites, lightly beaten
2   garlic cloves, minced and divided
Cooking spray
¼   cup light mayonnaise
1   tablespoon grated Parmesan cheese
2   medium tomatoes, thinly sliced (about
     ¾ pound)
3   tablespoons crushed saltine crackers
     (about 4 crackers)

1. Preheat oven to 375°.

2. Combine cooked angel hair pasta, ¼ cup basil, salt, pepper, eggs, egg whites, and 1 garlic clove, and stir well. Spoon pasta mixture into an 11- x

Green Pea Guacamole has 66% less fat than regular guacamole.

Squash Halves With
Sausage-Spinach Filling

7-inch baking dish coated with cooking spray.

3. Combine remaining ¼ cup basil, remaining garlic, mayonnaise, and cheese in a bowl; stir well.

4. Arrange half of tomato slices over pasta mixture; spread with half of mayonnaise mixture. Top with remaining tomato slices and spread with remaining mayonnaise mixture. Sprinkle with cracker crumbs. Bake at 375° for 25 minutes or until egg mixture is set. Let stand 10 minutes before slicing. Yield: 4 servings.

POINTS: 6; **Exchanges:** 2½ Starch, 1 Veg, 1 Fat, ½ Med-fat Meat
Per serving: CAL 300 (27% from fat); PRO 13.7g; FAT 9.1g (sat 1.8g); CARB 40.3g; FIB 2.9g; CHOL 113mg; IRON 2.6mg; SOD 412mg; CALC 55mg

Squash Halves With Sausage-Spinach Filling

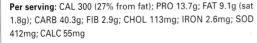

2   (1¾-pound) acorn squash
½   pound turkey Italian sausage
Cooking spray
½   cup chopped onion
½   cup sliced fresh mushrooms
2   tablespoons chopped red bell pepper
1   garlic clove, minced
1   (1-ounce) slice Italian bread, cubed
1   cup fresh spinach leaves
⅛   teaspoon pepper
4   teaspoons grated Parmesan cheese

1. Preheat oven to 350°.

2. Cut each squash in half lengthwise, and discard seeds and membrane. Place squash halves, cut side down, in a 13- x 9-inch baking dish. Cover and bake at 350° for 30 minutes. Uncover and set aside.

3. Cook sausage in a large nonstick skillet over medium-high heat until browned, stirring to crumble. Drain; set aside. Wipe drippings from skillet with a paper towel.

4. Coat skillet with cooking spray, and place over medium heat until hot. Add chopped onion and sliced mushrooms, and sauté 5 minutes. Add red bell pepper and minced garlic, and sauté 1 minute. Return sausage to skillet. Add bread cubes, spinach leaves, and pepper, and cook 3 minutes, stirring frequently.

5. Spoon about ½ cup sausage mixture into each squash half, and top each with 1 teaspoon cheese. Cover and bake at 350° for 45 minutes or until squash is tender. Yield: 4 servings.

POINTS: 4; **Exchanges:** 2 Starch, 1 Med-fat Meat
Per serving: CAL 240 (26% from fat); PRO 13.7g; FAT 7g (sat 2g); CARB 34.7g; FIB 4.5g; CHOL 37mg; IRON 3.2mg; SOD 396mg; CALC 140mg

Kale-and-Spinach Bake

2   teaspoons olive oil
1   cup finely chopped onion
2   garlic cloves, minced
10   cups chopped fresh kale (about 1 pound)
6½   cups chopped fresh spinach (about 1 pound)
Cooking spray
¾   cup plain low-fat yogurt
¼   cup grated Parmesan cheese
2½   tablespoons all-purpose flour
⅛   teaspoon salt
⅛   teaspoon ground nutmeg
⅛   teaspoon pepper
1   (16-ounce) carton 1% low-fat cottage cheese
2   large eggs
1   large egg white
1½   tablespoons grated Parmesan cheese

1. Heat olive oil in a Dutch oven over medium heat. Add chopped onion and minced garlic; sauté 3 minutes.

2. Stir in chopped kale and spinach. Reduce heat to medium-low; cover and cook 20 minutes, stirring occasionally. Remove from heat, and spoon into a 2-quart baking dish coated with cooking spray; set aside.

3. Preheat oven to 350°.

4. Place yogurt and next 8 ingredients in a food processor, and process until smooth. Pour yogurt mixture over greens, stirring gently. Sprinkle with grated Parmesan cheese. Bake, uncovered, at 350° for 40 minutes. Yield: 6 servings (serving size: 1 cup).

POINTS: 4; **Exchanges:** 2 Veg, 2 Very Lean Meat, 1 Starch, ½ Fat
Per serving: CAL 226 (27% from fat); PRO 21.4 g; FAT 6.9g (sat 2.5g); CARB 22.7g; FIB 4.6g; CHOL 79mg; IRON 4.1mg; SOD 586mg; CALC 384mg

Fantastic Fruits

An apple a day just isn't enough.

Full of fiber and cancer-fighting antioxidants,

fruit should be one of the staples of your diet.

---

*I*n Creative Writing 101, the first thing that would-be best-selling novelists are told is, "You have five senses—use them all." The same advice is invaluable when you're shopping for produce. You've got to look at, smell, listen to, touch, and taste fruit to make the best selections. Here's how it works: Of all fresh fruit, only passion fruit should be wrinkled; sickly sweet smelling fruit is past its prime; if you flick your finger on a melon, the thump should resonate; and, when no one's looking, the best test of all is to pop a grape or berry into your mouth. Sounds time consuming, but according to the experts, we should all linger a little longer on the produce aisle. An apple a day, they've discovered, just doesn't cut it. While we've always known that fruits and berries contain little sodium and no cholesterol but still pack in plenty of fiber, vitamins, and minerals, the current research buzzword is "antioxidants." Vitamins C and E and other antioxidants help prevent cancer by preventing fragments of molecules from forming cancer-causing chemicals, which explains why the American Cancer Society says we should eat at least five servings of fruits and vegetables every day. That's where we come in. This chapter includes more than 20 recipes featuring fantastic fruits, from Chicken Quesadillas With Papaya Salsa to Prosciutto and Pineapple Pizza, from Key Lime Pie to Apricot-Nut Bread. Get a cart—you'll never fit all that fruit in a basket.

This tangy Citrus Compote is the perfect finale to a winter meal.

Citrus Compote

4   small navel oranges
2   large red grapefruit
¾   cup water
¼   cup sugar
2   tablespoons triple sec (orange-flavored liqueur)
1   tablespoon grenadine

1. Remove rind from 2 oranges using a vegetable peeler (avoid the white pith of the rind). Cut orange rind into 1-inch strips to equal 3 tablespoons. Repeat procedure with 1 grapefruit.

2. Peel and section all oranges and grapefruit over a large bowl; squeeze membranes to extract juice. Set orange and grapefruit sections aside, reserving ¼ cup juice. Discard membranes.

3. Combine rind strips, water, and sugar in a small saucepan; bring to a boil. Cover, reduce heat, and simmer 2 minutes. Stir in reserved citrus juice, and simmer, uncovered, 10 minutes or until slightly thick. Remove from heat; stir in liqueur and grenadine. Pour mixture into a small bowl; cover and chill 30 minutes.

4. Arrange ¾ cup orange and grapefruit sections on each of 4 salad plates; drizzle ¼ cup juice mixture over each serving. Yield: 4 servings.

POINTS: 3; **Exchanges:** 2 Fruit, ½ Starch
Per serving: CAL 164 (2% from fat); PRO 1.7g; FAT 0.3g (sat 0g); CARB 37.6g; FIB 4g; CHOL 0mg; IRON 0.2mg; SOD 1mg; CALC 48mg

Fresh Blueberry Cobbler

4   cups fresh blueberries
1   teaspoon lemon juice
Cooking spray
1   cup all-purpose flour
½   cup sugar
1   teaspoon baking powder
⅛   teaspoon ground nutmeg
Dash of salt
1   tablespoon vegetable oil
½   teaspoon vanilla extract
2   large egg whites, lightly beaten
3   tablespoons sugar
½   teaspoon ground cinnamon

Dumpling-topped Fresh Blueberry Cobbler makes eight servings.

1. Preheat oven to 350°.

2. Combine blueberries and lemon juice in a 9-inch square baking dish coated with cooking spray; stir gently, and set aside.

3. Combine flour and next 4 ingredients in a large bowl; make a well in center of flour mixture. Combine oil, vanilla, and egg whites; stir well with a whisk. Add to flour mixture, stirring just until moist. Drop dough onto blueberry mixture to form 8 dumplings. Combine 3 tablespoons sugar and cinnamon, and sprinkle over dumplings. Bake at 350° for 35 minutes or until filling is bubbly and dumplings are lightly browned. Yield: 8 servings.

POINTS: 3; Exchanges: 1 Fruit, 1½ Starch
Per serving: CAL 186 (11% from fat); PRO 3g; FAT 2.2g (sat 0.4g); CARB 39.8g; FIB 3.7g; CHOL 0mg; IRON 1mg; SOD 22mg; CALC 43mg

Cherry-Almond Upside-Down Cake

1   tablespoon stick margarine, melted
¼   cup firmly packed brown sugar
3   tablespoons sliced almonds, toasted
1   (14.5-ounce) can unsweetened pitted tart or dark sweet cherries, drained
1¼   cups all-purpose flour
1   teaspoon baking powder
½   teaspoon baking soda
½   teaspoon salt
¼   cup stick margarine, softened
⅔   cup granulated sugar
1   teaspoon vanilla extract
½   teaspoon almond extract
1   large egg
½   cup low-fat buttermilk

1. Preheat oven to 350°.

2. Coat bottom of a 9-inch round cake pan with melted margarine. Sprinkle brown sugar and almonds over margarine. Arrange cherries over the brown sugar-almond mixture; set aside.

3. Combine flour and next 3 ingredients in a bowl; stir well. Combine ¼ cup margarine and granulated sugar in a large bowl; beat at medium speed of a mixer until well blended. Add extracts and egg; beat well. Add flour mixture to creamed

Cherry-Almond Upside-Down Cake

mixture alternately with buttermilk, beginning and ending with flour mixture; beat well after each addition. Pour batter over cherries.

4. Bake at 350° for 30 minutes or until a wooden pick inserted in center comes out clean. Let cool in pan 5 minutes on a wire rack. Loosen cake from sides of pan, using a narrow metal spatula. Invert onto a cake plate; cut into wedges. Serve warm. Yield: 8 servings.

POINTS: 6; Exchanges: 1½ Fat, 2 Starch, 1 Fruit
Per serving: CAL 277 (30% from fat); PRO 4.2g; FAT 9.3g (sat 1.9g); CARB 44.8g; FIB 0.9g; CHOL 28mg; IRON 1.5mg; SOD 329mg; CALC 79mg

Cherry-Rosemary Focaccia

Cherries and rosemary offer the perfect balance of sweet and savory flavors in this Italian bread. Serve it with roasted chicken or pork.

½   cup dried tart cherries
2   tablespoons water
1   (1-pound) loaf frozen white bread dough, thawed
2   teaspoons dried rosemary, crushed
Cooking spray
1   tablespoon extra-virgin olive oil or walnut oil

1. Combine cherries and water in a bowl; stir well, and let stand 30 minutes. Drain well.

2. Preheat oven to 400°.

3. Turn dough out onto a lightly floured surface; knead in cherries and rosemary. Pat dough into a 9-inch circle on a large baking sheet coated with

CHERRIES

There are two kinds of cherries: The sweet varieties that you eat out of hand, and the tart, sour varieties that are canned, frozen, juiced, and made into jams and pie fillings. Both are good sources of vitamin C and fiber.

Shopping

Buy brightly colored fruit that is shiny and plump. Sweet cherries, which are large and heart shaped, should be firm, but not hard. Sour cherries should be medium-firm. While cherries with stems keep longer, those without stems are cheaper.

Storage

Refrigerate unwashed cherries in a plastic bag for up to five days. Wash them just before using. You can freeze cherries without blanching them or removing the pits; they'll keep frozen for up to one year.

PAPAYAS

An excellent source of vitamin C and beta carotene, papaya contains papain, which tenderizes meat. To use papaya as a meat tenderizer, rub the puréed fruit over the meat, cover, and refrigerate for three hours. Scrape off the purée, pat the meat dry, and cook as desired.

Shopping

Look for golden-yellow fruit that gives slightly to palm pressure. Under-ripe papayas that are greenish in color ripen quickly at room temperature. To speed ripening, place in a paper bag with an apple. Pierce the bag several times with a knife, seal, and store at room temperature.

Storage

Ripe fruit should be stored in a plastic bag in the refrigerator and used within a week.

cooking spray. Cover and let rise in a warm place (85°), free from drafts, 15 minutes or until puffy.
4. Uncover dough. Dip the handle of a wooden spoon or your fingertips in flour and make indentations in the entire surface of the dough. Bake at 400° for 18 minutes or until lightly browned. Brush oil over surface of bread; cut into wedges. Serve warm. Yield: 8 servings.

POINTS: 3; **Exchanges:** 1½ Starch, ½ Fruit, ½ Fat
Per serving: CAL 170 (20% from fat); PRO 4.7g; FAT 3.7g (sat 0.2g); CARB 29.7g; FIB 2.3g; CHOL 0mg; IRON 1.7mg; SOD 258mg; CALC 43mg

Chicken Quesadillas With Papaya Salsa

Papaya Salsa
½   cup chopped cooked chicken breast
¼   cup chopped fresh cilantro
2   tablespoons fresh lime juice
2   tablespoons drained canned chopped chipotle chile in adobo sauce
1   tablespoon chopped onion
4   (8-inch) fat-free flour tortillas
1½ cups (6 ounces) shredded reduced-fat Monterey Jack cheese
Cooking spray
1   teaspoon vegetable oil, divided

1. Prepare Papaya Salsa. Cover; chill 30 minutes.
2. Combine chicken and next 4 ingredients in a bowl; stir well. Spoon chicken mixture evenly onto each tortilla. Sprinkle evenly with cheese, and fold in half.
3. Coat a large nonstick skillet with cooking spray; add ½ teaspoon oil, and place over medium-high heat until hot. Add 2 quesadillas; cook 1 minute on each side or until lightly browned. Remove from skillet; set aside, and keep warm. Repeat procedure with remaining oil and quesadillas. Cut each quesadilla in half, and serve with Papaya Salsa. Yield: 4 servings (serving size: 1 quesadilla and ½ cup Papaya Salsa).

Papaya Salsa:
2   cups peeled chopped papaya
¼   cup chopped onion
¼   cup chopped fresh cilantro

2   tablespoons fresh lime juice
2   teaspoons finely chopped jalapeño pepper
⅛   teaspoon salt

1. Combine all ingredients in a medium bowl; stir well. Stir before serving. Yield: 2 cups (serving size: ½ cup).

POINTS: 6; **Exchanges:** 2 Starch, 1½ Med-fat Meat, ½ Very Lean Meat, ½ Fruit
Per serving: CAL 317 (29% from fat); PRO 20.8g; FAT 10.3g (sat 5.2g); CARB 35.8g; FIB 3.6g; CHOL 40mg; IRON 1.9mg; SOD 797mg; CALC 374mg

Papaya Lemonade

1   cup sugar
1   cup boiling water
3½ cups cold water, divided
3   cups peeled chopped papaya
1   cup fresh lemon juice (about 4 large lemons)

1. Combine sugar and boiling water, stirring until sugar dissolves. Let cool slightly. Place sugar syrup, 2 cups cold water, papaya, and lemon juice in a blender; process until mixture is smooth. Stir in remaining 1½ cups water. Serve over ice. Yield: 8 servings (serving size: 1 cup).

POINTS: 2; **Exchanges:** 2 Fruit
Per serving: CAL 125 (1% from fat); PRO 0.4g; FAT 0.1g (sat 0g); CARB 32.8g; FIB 0.9g; CHOL 0mg; IRON 0.1mg; SOD 2mg; CALC 15mg

Citrus-Shrimp Salad

To make ahead, arrange Citrus-Shrimp Salad on a platter 1 to 2 hours before serving. Cover with plastic wrap, and chill.

2   pounds medium shrimp
¼   cup fat-free Italian dressing
3   tablespoons finely chopped shallots
2   tablespoons red wine vinegar
2   tablespoons orange juice
2   tablespoons plain fat-free yogurt
1½ tablespoons Dijon mustard
1   tablespoon honey
⅛   teaspoon pepper
4   cups sliced romaine lettuce
2   cups pink grapefruit sections (about 4 large grapefruit)
2   cups orange sections (about 5 oranges)
¼   cup chopped fresh chives

Citrus-Shrimp Salad

Papaya-Pineapple Kabobs With Golden Caramel Sauce is a colorful ending to any meal.

1. Bring 2½ quarts water to a boil in a large saucepan. Add shrimp, and cook 3 minutes or until done. Drain and rinse under cold water. Peel and chill shrimp.

2. Combine Italian dressing and next 7 ingredients in a large bowl; stir well. Stir in shrimp.

3. Line a large platter with sliced romaine lettuce. Spoon shrimp mixture into center of platter, and arrange grapefruit and orange sections around salad. Sprinkle salad with chopped chives. Yield: 8 servings.

POINTS: 2; **Exchanges:** 1 Fruit, 2½ Very Lean Meat
Per serving: CAL 147 (8% from fat); PRO 19.4g; FAT 1.3g (sat 0.3g); CARB 14.4g; FIB 2.9g; CHOL 166mg; IRON 3.1mg; SOD 350mg; CALC 78mg

Papaya-Pineapple Kabobs With Golden Caramel Sauce

Cooked under a broiler or grilled, this dessert adds a sprightly taste to either brunch or dinner.

3 cups peeled cubed papaya, divided
¼ cup fresh lime juice
2 tablespoons dark rum
2 teaspoons vanilla extract
1 cup water
¾ cup firmly packed brown sugar
3 whole cloves
1 (4-inch) cinnamon stick
3 cups cubed fresh pineapple
Cooking spray

1. Place ¾ cup papaya, lime juice, rum, and vanilla in a food processor, and process until smooth; set aside.

2. Combine water, sugar, cloves, and cinnamon in a medium saucepan; cook over medium heat 13 minutes. Increase heat to medium-high; cook an additional 10 minutes or until mixture is the consistency of thin syrup (do not stir). Remove from heat; let stand 1 minute. Discard cloves and cinnamon stick. Carefully stir in puréed papaya mixture. Pour sauce into a bowl; set aside.

Teriyaki Tuna With Fresh Pineapple

3. Prepare grill or broiler. Thread remaining papaya cubes and pineapple cubes alternately onto each of 6 (10-inch) skewers. Place skewers on grill rack or broiler pan coated with cooking spray; grill or broil 8 minutes or until lightly browned, turning and basting occasionally with caramel sauce. Serve kabobs with remaining sauce. Yield: 6 servings (serving size: 1 kabob and 3 tablespoons sauce).

POINTS: 3; **Exchanges:** 3 Fruit
Per serving: CAL 177 (3% from fat); PRO 0.8g; FAT 0.6g (sat 0.1g); CARB 44.4g; FIB 2.4g; CHOL 0mg; IRON 0.9mg; SOD 14mg; CALC 48mg

Teriyaki Tuna With Fresh Pineapple

¼   cup low-salt soy sauce
3   tablespoons honey
3   tablespoons mirin (sweet rice wine)
2   teaspoons peeled minced fresh ginger
½   teaspoon hot sauce
1   garlic clove, minced
1   small ripe fresh pineapple, peeled and cored
6   (4-ounce) tuna steaks (about ¾ inch thick)
Cooking spray
Green onions (optional)

1. Combine first 6 ingredients in a large shallow dish. Cut pineapple lengthwise into 6 spears. Add pineapple and tuna to soy sauce mixture, turning to coat. Cover and marinate in refrigerator 30 minutes, turning every 10 minutes.

2. Prepare grill. Remove tuna steaks and pineapple from dish, reserving marinade. Place tuna and pineapple on grill rack coated with cooking spray, and grill 4 minutes on each side or until tuna is desired degree of doneness, basting tuna and pineapple occasionally with reserved marinade. Garnish with green onions, if desired. Yield: 6 servings (serving size: 1 tuna steak and 1 pineapple spear).

POINTS: 5; **Exchanges:** 4 Very Lean Meat, 1½ Fruit
Per serving: CAL 249 (22% from fat); PRO 27.4g; FAT 6.1g (sat 1.5g); CARB 21.5g; FIB 1.4g; CHOL 43mg; IRON 1.8mg; SOD 371mg; CALC 10mg

Prosciutto-and-Pineapple Pizza

1   whole garlic head
1   tablespoon prepared pesto (such as Pesto Sanremo)
2   (8-ounce) cans pineapple tidbits, drained
1   (10-ounce) can refrigerated pizza crust dough (such as Pillsbury)
Cooking spray
3   ounces thinly sliced prosciutto, chopped
¼   cup (1 ounce) shredded fontina cheese
¼   cup (1 ounce) shredded fresh Parmesan cheese
1   tablespoon pine nuts

1. Preheat oven to 425°.

2. Remove thin white, papery skin from whole garlic head (do not peel or separate cloves). Wrap garlic head in aluminum foil. Bake at 425° for 30 minutes or until tender; let cool 10 minutes.

3. Separate cloves; squeeze to extract garlic pulp. Discard skins. Combine roasted garlic pulp and prepared pesto in a small bowl; stir mixture well, and set aside.

4. Place pineapple tidbits on several layers of paper towels, spreading in a single layer; cover with additional paper towels, pressing gently to remove excess moisture.

5. Unroll pizza crust dough onto a baking sheet coated with cooking spray. Pat dough into a 12- x 10-inch rectangle. Spread pesto mixture over dough, and top with pineapple tidbits and chopped prosciutto. Sprinkle with

Pineapple is a fair source of vitamins A and C. Like papaya, it can be used to tenderize meat. Most often eaten raw, pineapple is delicious cooked—whether it is sautéed, grilled, broiled, or incorporated into a dessert recipe, such as pineapple upside-down cake.

Shopping

Look for pineapples that are slightly soft with no signs of greening. The leaves should be crisp and green with no yellow or brown tips. If the base of the fruit smells sweet and you can easily pull a leaf from its crown, it's ripe.

Storage

Tightly wrap whole, ripe pineapple and refrigerate for up to three days. Sliced pineapple can be refrigerated, wrapped, for up to three more days.

shredded fontina and Parmesan cheeses and pine nuts. Bake pizza at 425° for 10 minutes or until crust is lightly browned. Yield: 5 servings (serving size: 1 slice).

POINTS: 7; **Exchanges:** 2 Starch, 1 Fruit, 1 Hi-fat Meat
Per serving: CAL 320 (30% from fat); PRO 13.6g; FAT 10.6g (sat 3.1g); CARB 42.3g; FIB 1.6g; CHOL 21mg; IRON 2.1mg; SOD 702mg; CALC 127mg

Chicken-and-French Bean Salad With Blueberry Relish

You can make the vinaigrette and relish ahead of time and then cook the chicken breast halves just before serving the salad.

1 cup (2-inch) cut fresh green beans (about ¼ pound)
¾ cup fresh blueberries
1 tablespoon sugar
2 tablespoons balsamic vinegar
2 tablespoons chopped red onion
2 teaspoons fresh lemon juice
3 tablespoons red wine vinegar
1 tablespoon chopped shallots
2 teaspoons honey mustard
2 teaspoons olive oil, divided
¼ teaspoon salt
¼ teaspoon pepper

Chicken-and-French Bean Salad With Blueberry Relish is best served at room temperature.

2 (4-ounce) skinned, boned chicken breast halves
2 cups torn romaine lettuce
1 cup plain croutons

1. Steam green beans, covered, 5 minutes or until crisp-tender. Rinse beans under cold water; drain and set aside.

2. Place blueberries and next 4 ingredients in a food processor; pulse until coarsely chopped. Set relish aside.

3. Combine red wine vinegar, chopped shallots, honey mustard, and 1 teaspoon olive oil in a small bowl; stir with a whisk until well blended. Set vinaigrette aside.

4. Sprinkle salt and pepper over chicken breasts. Heat remaining 1 teaspoon oil in a small nonstick skillet over medium heat. Add chicken, and cook 3 minutes on each side or until done. Remove from heat, and cut across grain into thin slices; set aside.

5. Combine green beans, romaine lettuce, and croutons in a medium bowl. Drizzle vinaigrette over salad, and toss gently to coat. Divide salad evenly between 2 plates, and top each with chicken breast slices. Spoon relish over chicken. Yield: 2 servings.

POINTS: 7; **Exchanges:** 2 Starch, 2 Veg, 2 Very Lean Meat, 2 Fat
Per serving: CAL 372 (27% from fat); PRO 25.4g; FAT 11.1g (sat 2.2g); CARB 42g; FIB 4.9g; CHOL 49mg; IRON 2.5mg; SOD 426mg; CALC 83mg

Chicken in Citrus Sauce

Based on a classic French recipe, the citrus sauce is delicious with pork chops, game hens, and turkey thighs.

½ cup water
2 tablespoons (½-inch) julienne-cut orange rind
1 tablespoon (½-inch) julienne-cut grapefruit rind
2 teaspoons (½-inch) julienne-cut lemon rind
1 teaspoon (½-inch) julienne-cut lime rind
¾ cup low-salt chicken broth
¾ cup fresh orange juice

¼ cup dry red wine
2 tablespoons fresh grapefruit juice
2 teaspoons fresh lemon juice
2 teaspoons fresh lime juice
1 teaspoon sugar
¼ teaspoon salt
¼ teaspoon pepper
8 chicken thighs (about 3 pounds),
  skinned
1 teaspoon margarine
1 tablespoon white wine vinegar
½ teaspoon cornstarch

1. Combine water and next 4 ingredients in a small saucepan; bring to a boil. Cover, reduce heat, and simmer 10 minutes; drain, reserving citrus rind. Combine citrus rind, chicken broth, and next 6 ingredients in a small bowl. Stir well, and set aside.

2. Sprinkle salt and pepper over chicken thighs. Heat margarine in a large nonstick skillet over medium-high heat. Add chicken, and cook 3 minutes on each side. Add broth mixture; cover, reduce heat, and simmer 35 minutes. Remove chicken from skillet with a slotted spoon; set aside, and keep warm.

3. Combine white wine vinegar and cornstarch; stir well. Add cornstarch mixture to broth mixture in skillet, and simmer, uncovered, 10 minutes or until mixture is thick and slightly reduced, stirring constantly. Spoon sauce over chicken. Yield: 4 servings (serving size: 2 chicken thighs and ¼ cup sauce).

POINTS: 4; **Exchanges:** ½ Starch, 3 Lean Meat
Per serving: CAL 198 (29% from fat); PRO 26g; FAT 6.3g (sat 1.5g); CARB 9.8g; FIB 0.2g; CHOL 106 mg; IRON 1.9mg; SOD 284mg; CALC 29mg

Apricot-Nut Bread

For variety when making this bread, you may use dates, raisins, or prunes instead of apricots and still get the same delicious flavor.

2½ cups all-purpose flour
1 cup chopped dried apricots
⅔ cup sugar
½ cup chopped walnuts
1 tablespoon baking powder

1 teaspoon salt
4 teaspoons grated orange rind
1 cup fresh orange juice
½ cup 1% low-fat milk
3 tablespoons applesauce
2 large egg whites, lightly beaten
Cooking spray

1. Preheat oven to 350°.

2. Combine first 7 ingredients in a large bowl, and make a well in center of flour mixture. Combine fresh orange juice, low-fat milk, applesauce, and egg whites in a small bowl; add orange juice mixture to flour mixture, stirring just until moist.

3. Pour batter into a 9- x 5-inch loaf pan coated with cooking spray. Bake at 350° for 1 hour or until a wooden pick inserted in center comes out clean.

4. Remove from pan, and let cool on a wire rack. Yield: 16 servings.

POINTS: 3; **Exchanges:** 1½ Starch, ½ Fat
Per serving: CAL 140 (17% from fat); PRO 3.7g; FAT 2.6g (sat 0.2g); CARB 26.3g; FIB 1g; CHOL 0mg; IRON 1.1mg; SOD 158mg; CALC 52mg

For quick cleanup, use scissors to chop the dried fruit in Apricot-Nut Bread.

Key Lime Pie

Apple, Caramelized Onion, and Brie Calzones

We tested this recipe with McIntosh apples, but you can substitute any sweet, red cooking apple. Leave the skin on for color and to allow the apple slices to hold their shape.

Olive oil-flavored cooking spray
1   teaspoon olive oil
4   cups thinly sliced Vidalia or other sweet onion
½   teaspoon dried thyme
1   (1-pound) loaf frozen white bread dough, thawed
2   cups sliced red cooking apple
1   cup (½-inch) cubed Brie cheese (about 5 ounces)

1. Coat a nonstick skillet with cooking spray; add olive oil, and place over medium heat. Add onion, and cook 1 minute. Reduce heat to medium-low; add thyme. Cook 20 minutes, stirring occasionally.

2. Preheat oven to 400°.

3. Divide white bread dough into 7 equal portions. Working with 1 portion at a time (cover remaining dough to keep it from drying), roll each portion into a 7-inch circle on a lightly floured surface.

4. Divide onion mixture evenly among bread dough circles. Arrange apple slices evenly over onion mixture, overlapping slightly. Top with cheese. Moisten edges of dough with water, and fold dough over filling. Press edges together with a fork to seal.

5. Place calzones on a baking sheet coated with cooking spray. Lightly coat calzones with cooking spray. Bake at 400° for 12 minutes or until golden. Serve warm or at room temperature. Yield: 7 servings.

Note: We found partially freezing the Brie made it easier to cube. Blue cheese may be substituted if a more pungent flavor is desired.

POINTS: 5; **Exchanges:** 2½ Starch, ½ Hi-fat Meat
Per serving: CAL 265 (25% from fat); PRO 9.7g; FAT 7.4g (sat 3g); CARB 40.7g; FIB 4.8g; CHOL 16mg; IRON 1.8mg; SOD 400mg; CALC 87mg

> **O**ne serving equals a medium-size fruit, ½ cup fruit, or ¾ cup juice.

Key Lime Pie

1   teaspoon unflavored gelatin
2   tablespoons cold water
½   cup fresh lime juice
2   large egg yolks
1   (14-ounce) can fat-free sweetened condensed milk
Graham Cracker Crust
3   large egg whites (at room temperature)
¼   teaspoon cream of tartar
⅛   teaspoon salt
⅓   cup sugar
Lime slices (optional)

1. Preheat oven to 325°.

2. Sprinkle gelatin over cold water in a small bowl, and set aside. Combine lime juice and egg yolks in a small, heavy saucepan; cook over medium-low heat 10 minutes or until slightly thick and very hot (180°), stirring constantly (do not boil). Add softened, unflavored gelatin to lime juice mixture, and cook 1 minute, stirring until gelatin completely dissolves. Place saucepan in a large ice-filled bowl, and stir gelatin mixture 3 minutes or until room temperature (do not allow gelatin mixture to set). Strain gelatin mixture through a sieve into a medium bowl, and discard solids. Gradually add milk, stirring with a whisk until blended (mixture will be very thick), and spoon mixture into Graham Cracker Crust, spreading evenly.

3. Beat egg whites, cream of tartar, and salt at high speed of a mixer until foamy. Gradually add sugar, 1 tablespoon at a time, beating until stiff peaks form. Spread meringue evenly over pie filling, sealing to edge of crust.

4. Bake at 325° for 25 minutes; let cool 1 hour on a wire rack. Chill 3 hours or until set. Cut with a sharp knife dipped in hot water. Garnish with lime slices, if desired. Yield: 8 servings.

POINTS: 6; **Exchanges:** 4 Starch
Per serving: CAL 290 (14% from fat); PRO 7.5g; FAT 4.4g (sat 1.1g); CARB 65.1g; FIB 0.1g; CHOL 61mg; IRON 0.9mg; SOD 230mg; CALC 118mg

CRANBERRIES

Fresh cranberries, which are very high in vitamin C, are 90% water. The remaining 10% is carbohydrates and fiber. Often thought of as merely a Thanksgiving side dish, cranberries also make delicious chutneys, pies, and cobblers.

Shopping

Cranberries are often sold in 12-ounce bags, so you can't pick them individually, but look for vivid-red berries. Before using or freezing cranberries, discard any berries that are wrinkled, discolored, or soft, and remove any stems.

Storage

Cranberries can be stored in an airtight plastic bag in the refrigerator for up to two months. They can be frozen for up to one year and can be used directly from the freezer without thawing.

Graham Cracker Crust:

2   tablespoons sugar
1   tablespoon chilled stick margarine
1   large egg white
1¼ cups graham cracker crumbs
1   teaspoon ground cinnamon
Cooking spray

1. Preheat oven to 325°.

2. Combine first 3 ingredients in a bowl; beat at medium speed of a mixer. Add crumbs and cinnamon; toss with a fork until moist. Press into a 9-inch pie plate coated with cooking spray. Bake at 325° for 20 minutes or until lightly browned; let cool on a wire rack. Yield: 1 (9-inch) crust.

Strawberry Chutney

Our taste-testing panel enjoyed this condiment served on Carr's table water crackers with a choice of Brie and light cream cheese.

¼   cup raisins
¼   cup firmly packed brown sugar
¼   cup fresh lemon juice
¼   cup raspberry vinegar
2   tablespoons honey
2   cups sliced fresh strawberries

1. Combine first 5 ingredients in a saucepan; bring to a boil. Reduce heat to medium, and cook 15 minutes or until slightly thick. Stir in strawberries. Reduce heat to low, and simmer 10 minutes or until thick, stirring occasionally. Yield: 1 cup (serving size: 1 tablespoon).

POINTS: 1; *Exchanges:* ½ Fruit
Per serving: CAL 35 (3% from fat); PRO 0.2g; FAT 0.1g (sat 0g); CARB 9.1g; FIB 0.6g; CHOL 0mg; IRON 0.2mg; SOD 2mg; CALC 7mg

Cranberry-Chocolate Crumble

¾   cup water
½   cup granulated sugar
1   (12-ounce) bag fresh cranberries
⅓   cup seedless raspberry jam
Cooking spray
2   tablespoons milk chocolate chips
½   cup all-purpose flour
⅓   cup regular oats
  ¼   cup firmly packed brown sugar
  3   tablespoons stick margarine, melted

1. Preheat oven to 350°.

2. Combine water, granulated sugar, and cranberries in a saucepan; bring to a boil. Reduce heat, and simmer 10 minutes, stirring occasionally. Remove from heat, and stir in jam. Divide mixture evenly among 6 (6-ounce) custard cups coated with cooking spray, and sprinkle with chocolate chips.

3. Combine flour, oats, brown sugar, and margarine; toss well. Sprinkle oat mixture evenly over cranberry mixture. Place cups on a baking sheet; bake at 350° for 20 minutes or until bubbly. Yield: 6 servings.

POINTS: 6; *Exchanges:* 2½ Starch, 1½ Fat, 1 Fruit
Per serving: CAL 305 (22% from fat); PRO 2.5g; FAT 7.6g (sat 2g); CARB 58.6g; FIB 1.5g; CHOL 2mg; IRON 1mg; SOD 82mg; CALC 19mg

Port-Marinated Tenderloin With Cranberries

Leftovers from this tenderloin make a great sandwich filling.

1   (3-pound) beef tenderloin
1   cup dried cranberries
1   cup cranberry juice cocktail
1   cup tawny port
3   tablespoons brown sugar
2   tablespoons low-salt soy sauce
1   teaspoon coarsely ground pepper
¼   teaspoon salt
3   garlic cloves, minced
Cooking spray
1   tablespoon all-purpose flour
Thyme sprigs (optional)

1. Trim fat from tenderloin. Combine tenderloin and next 8 ingredients in a large zip-top plastic bag. Seal bag, and marinate in refrigerator 24 hours, turning bag occasionally. Remove tenderloin from bag, reserving marinade.

2. Preheat oven to 500°.

3. Place tenderloin on a broiler pan coated with cooking spray. Insert meat thermometer into thickest portion of tenderloin. Place in oven, and immediately reduce oven temperature to 350°. Bake at 350° for 1 hour and 10 minutes or until

thermometer registers 145° (medium-rare) to 160° (medium). Let stand 10 minutes.

4. Combine flour and 2 tablespoons reserved marinade in a skillet; stir with a whisk. Add remaining marinade to skillet, stirring with a whisk. Bring to a boil; cook 8 minutes or until thick, stirring constantly.

5. Serve sauce warm with tenderloin. Garnish with thyme sprigs, if desired. Yield: 12 servings (serving size: 3 ounces beef and about 2 tablespoons sauce).

Note: Squeeze the excess air out of the zip-top plastic bag before sealing so the marinade completely surrounds the entire piece of meat. For easy cleanup, line broiler pan with foil. This way, the juices won't bake onto pan.

POINTS: 4; **Exchanges:** 2 Lean Meat, 1 Starch
Per serving: CAL 201 (21% from fat); PRO 14.8g; FAT 4.8g (sat 1.8g); CARB 19.6g; FIB 0.7g; CHOL 42mg; IRON 2.4mg; SOD 166mg; CALC 16mg

Jamaican Jerk Roasted Chicken and Bananas

¼	cup plain fat-free yogurt
1	teaspoon sugar
1	teaspoon ground allspice
½	teaspoon salt
½	teaspoon dried thyme
½	teaspoon ground red pepper
¼	teaspoon ground mace
¼	teaspoon ground nutmeg
¼	teaspoon black pepper
1	(5- to 6-pound) roasting chicken
4	medium unripe bananas, peeled and cut in half lengthwise
1	tablespoon all-purpose flour
1	cup low-salt chicken broth
½	cup orange juice
2	tablespoons dark rum

1. Preheat oven to 450°.

2. Combine first 9 ingredients; stir well. Set aside.

3. Discard giblets and neck from chicken. Rinse chicken under cold water; pat dry, and trim fat.

Yorkshire pudding and julienne carrots complement Port-Marinated Tenderloin With Cranberries.

APRICOTS

Apricots are rich in beta carotene, a potent antioxidant. The riper the fruit, the higher the beta carotene content. Apricots also are high in soluble fiber and contain potassium and vitamin C (most of which is found near the skin, so don't peel apricots).

Shopping

Look for plump apricots with evenly colored, orange-gold skin. Hard fruit tinged with green won't fully ripen.

Storage

Store-bought apricots usually need ripening; place them in a paper bag at room temperature away from heat and direct sun. After ripening, unwashed apricots can be refrigerated in a plastic bag for up to three days.

Fresh Apricot Jam

Starting at neck cavity, loosen skin from breast and drumsticks by inserting fingers and gently pushing between skin and meat. Spread yogurt mixture under loosened skin. Lift wing tips up and over back; tuck under chicken.

4. Place chicken, breast side up, on a broiler pan. Insert meat thermometer into meaty part of thigh, making sure not to touch bone. Bake at 450° for 20 minutes. Reduce oven temperature to 350°. Arrange bananas around chicken, and bake an additional 1 hour and 30 minutes or until thermometer registers 180°. Discard skin.

5. Set chicken and bananas aside; keep warm. Pour pan drippings into a small zip-top plastic bag. Snip off 1 small corner of the bag, and drain liquid into a saucepan, stopping before the fat layer reaches the opening. Discard fat.

6. Place flour in a small bowl; gradually add broth, stirring with a whisk. Add to pan drippings in saucepan, and stir in orange juice and rum. Bring to a boil, and cook 1 minute or until thick, stirring constantly with a whisk. Serve with chicken and bananas. Yield: 8 servings (serving size: 3 ounces chicken, 1 banana half, and 3 tablespoons gravy).

POINTS: 5; **Exchanges:** 1 Starch, 1 Very Lean Meat, 2 Lean Meat, ½ Fruit
Per serving: CAL 249 (25% from fat); PRO 26.1g; FAT 6.9g (sat 1.9g); CARB 18g; FIB 1.9g; CHOL 76mg; IRON 1.6mg; SOD 290mg; CALC 36mg

Fresh Apricot Jam

6 cups coarsely chopped fresh apricots (about 2 pounds)
3 cups sugar
2 tablespoons fresh lemon juice

1. Combine all ingredients in a large bowl, and stir well. Cover and let stand at room temperature 24 hours.

2. Spoon apricot mixture into a large saucepan, and bring to a boil over medium heat, stirring frequently. Reduce heat to low, and cook, uncovered, 25 minutes or until candy thermometer registers 205°. Pour jam into hot decorative jars or airtight containers, and store in refrigerator for up to 3 weeks. Yield: 4 cups (serving size: 1 tablespoon).

Note: If you shy away from canning your own jams and jellies, this easy recipe will make "homemade" a little less intimidating.

POINTS: 1; **Exchanges:** ½ Starch
Per serving: CAL 43 (2% from fat); PRO 0.2g; FAT 0.1g (sat 0g); CARB 11g; FIB 0.3g; CHOL 0mg; IRON 0.1mg; SOD 0mg; CALC 2mg

New England-Style Bananas Foster

⅓ cup maple syrup
⅓ cup dark rum
3½ cups diagonally sliced firm ripe banana
⅓ cup chopped walnuts, toasted
3 cups vanilla fat-free frozen yogurt

1. Combine maple syrup and dark rum in a large nonstick skillet, and bring to a simmer over medium-low heat. Add sliced banana to syrup mixture, and cook 3 minutes, stirring occasionally. Add chopped walnuts, and cook 1 minute. Serve immediately over frozen yogurt. Yield: 6 servings (serving size: ½ cup banana mixture and ½ cup frozen yogurt).

Note: Be careful not to overcook the banana mixture or it will turn dark.

POINTS: 6; **Exchanges:** 2½ Starch, 1 Fruit, 1 Fat
Per serving: CAL 296 (13% from fat); PRO 6.2g; FAT 4.4g (sat 0.4g); CARB 51.9g; FIB 3g; CHOL 0mg; IRON 0.7mg; SOD 65mg; CALC 156mg

New England-Style
Bananas Foster

Magical Beans

Once we understand the nutritional power of legumes,
Jack of fee-fi-fo-fum fame might seem a little less foolish.

As children we pitied little Jack, a poor country boy who traded the family cow for a handful of magic beans. Silly Jack, we thought, surely he'll be punished. What we—and Jack's mother—didn't understand then is that beans truly are magical—nutritionally speaking, that is. Not only are beans cholesterol-free, but they also have been proven to lower your blood-cholesterol level. Here's how it works: Beans contain gums and pectin, soluble dietary fibers that mop up fats and prevent their absorption by your body. But that's not all. Beans also protect diabetics from blood-sugar overload. Since they're digested slowly, they produce only a gradual increase in the level of sugar circulating in your blood. So when you eat beans, your body needs less insulin than when you eat other high-carb foods such as pasta and potatoes. In a University of Kentucky study, a bean-rich diet made it possible for people with Type I diabetes to reduce their daily insulin intake by nearly 40% and those with Type II by 98%. Beans are high in fiber, low in fat, and a good source of iron, folic acid, and potassium. And when combined with rice or pasta, beans supply all the amino acids a body needs. Maybe Jack was ahead of his time. Maybe that's why he ended up the hero.

Nonnie's Spaghini Stick-to-Your Ribs Soup brings together a variety of healthy ingredients.

Nonnie's Spaghini Stick-to-Your-Ribs Soup

1 pound ground round
5 cups water
4 cups chopped green cabbage (about 1 pound)
3½ cups tomato juice
1 tablespoon dried oregano
1½ teaspoons garlic powder
1½ teaspoons pepper
1 teaspoon salt
¼ teaspoon dried thyme
3 (15-ounce) cans kidney beans, drained
3 (14.5-ounce) cans diced tomatoes, undrained
2 (14¼-ounce) cans fat-free beef broth
8 ounces uncooked angel hair pasta

1. Cook beef in a 12-quart Dutch oven or stockpot over medium heat until browned, stirring to crumble. Drain well, and return to pan.

2. Add water and next 10 ingredients; bring to a boil. Reduce heat, and simmer, uncovered, 2 hours, stirring occasionally.

3. Break pasta in half; stir into soup, and cook an additional 5 minutes or until pasta is done. Yield: 13 servings (serving size: 1½ cups).

POINTS: 3; **Exchanges:** 1 Starch, 1 Veg, 1 Lean Meat
Per serving: CAL 163 (10% from fat); PRO 14.7g; FAT 1.9g (sat 0.6g); CARB 22.8g; FIB 3.3g; CHOL 19mg; IRON 3.4mg; SOD 625mg; CALC 59mg

Steak-and-Black-eyed Pea Salad

1 (12-ounce) lean flank steak
1 tablespoon spicy brown mustard
½ teaspoon garlic powder
¼ teaspoon pepper
Cooking spray
5 cups torn romaine lettuce
1 cup cherry tomatoes, halved
1 cup (¼-inch-thick) sliced cucumber
½ cup sliced onion, separated into rings
1 (15-ounce) can black-eyed peas, rinsed and drained
¾ cup fat-free Italian dressing

1. Prepare grill or broiler.

2. Trim fat from steak. Combine mustard, garlic powder, and pepper; spread over both sides of steak. Place steak on a grill rack or broiler pan coated with cooking spray; grill or broil 5 minutes on each side. Cut steak diagonally across grain into thin slices.

3. Combine steak, lettuce, tomatoes, cucumber, onion, and black-eyed peas in a bowl. Drizzle dressing over salad; toss well. Yield: 4 servings (serving size: 2 cups).

Note: Substitute 1 (16-ounce) can cannellini beans for black-eyed peas, if desired.

POINTS: 7; **Exchanges:** 2 Veg, 2 Med-fat Meat, 1½ Starch
Per serving: CAL 323 (34% from fat); PRO 24.6g; FAT 12.1g (sat 4.3g); CARB 29.1g; FIB 4.7g; CHOL 45mg; IRON 4.8mg; SOD 679mg; CALC 76mg

BEAN BASICS

Dried Beans

Cooking

Before cooking dried beans, inspect them thoroughly, and remove any pebbles or other debris. Most dried beans need to be soaked before cooking. One pound is equivalent to about 2½ cups uncooked or 5½ to 6½ cups cooked.

Soaking

The Traditional Method: Soak beans in water for as many as eight hours to rehydrate them. Use 10 cups of cold water for every 2 cups (1 pound) of dried beans. Drain off the soaking water and add fresh water to cook the beans.

The Quick Soak Method: If you don't have time to soak beans overnight, put them in a large pot, add 10 cups of hot water for every 2 cups (1 pound) of dried beans, and bring them to a boil for 1 to 2 minutes. Remove pot from heat; cover and let stand 1 to 2 hours. Drain and add fresh water to cook

Canned Beans

Cooking

Contrary to popular belief, canned beans are just as good for you as the fresh and dried varieties because they are canned just a few hours after they're picked, sealing in nutrients. You may drain and rinse canned beans before cooking to remove any excess salt. Although they're still very economical, canned beans are more expensive than dried beans. One 15-ounce can yields about 1¾ cups of drained beans.

Fresh Beans

Storage

Refrigerate unshelled fresh beans in an unsealed plastic bag for several days; cover shelled beans with plastic wrap and refrigerate for up to two days.

Cooking

Remove fresh beans from their shells and boil for 10 minutes.

John's Hot-and-Hoppin' Cavatappi

Be sure to use the hot pepper sauce that contains whole peppers packed in vinegar. Red-colored hot sauce won't yield good results.

2   cups water
1½ cups frozen black-eyed peas, thawed
1   teaspoon dried thyme
2   bay leaves
½   cup chopped sun-dried tomatoes, packed without oil
1½ teaspoons hot pepper sauce (such as Cajun Chef)
4   cups hot cooked cavatappi (about 6 ounces uncooked spiral-shaped pasta)
½   cup sliced green onions
½   cup chopped fresh parsley
3   ounces very thinly sliced prosciutto or lean ham, chopped
¼   cup hot pepper sauce (such as Cajun Chef)
2   tablespoons finely chopped fresh green chiles or canned chopped green chiles, drained
1   tablespoon extra-virgin olive oil
½   teaspoon dry mustard
3   garlic cloves, minced

1. Combine first 4 ingredients in a saucepan; bring to a boil. Cover, reduce heat, and simmer 15 minutes or until tender. Add tomatoes and 1½ teaspoons pepper sauce; simmer 5 minutes or until tomatoes are tender. Drain black-eyed pea mixture in a colander over a bowl, reserving 2 tablespoons cooking liquid. Discard bay leaves.

2. Combine black-eyed pea mixture, pasta, green onions, parsley, and prosciutto. Combine reserved cooking liquid, ¼ cup pepper sauce, and next 4 ingredients; stir well with a whisk. Pour pepper sauce mixture over pasta mixture; toss well. Serve warm or at room temperature. Yield: 4 servings (serving size: 1½ cups).

POINTS: 5; **Exchanges:** 2½ Starch, 1 Veg, ½ Fat
Per serving: CAL 246 (16% from fat); PRO 12.5g; FAT 4.5g (sat 0.8g); CARB 40.2g; FIB 2.7g; CHOL 8mg; IRON 3mg; SOD 443mg; CALC 51mg

Steak-and-Black-eyed Pea Salad is ready to serve in 20 minutes or less.

Tex-Mex Tofu Burritos

Tex-Mex Tofu Burritos

1   (10.5-ounce) package reduced-fat extra-firm tofu, drained and cut into ½-inch cubes
1   teaspoon ground cumin
1   teaspoon chili powder
2   teaspoons cider vinegar
½   teaspoon ground cinnamon
2   teaspoons vegetable oil
1   cup sliced onion, separated into rings
1   cup (3- x ¼-inch) julienne-cut red bell pepper
1   cup (3- x ¼-inch) julienne-cut zucchini
½   cup corn, black bean, and roasted-red pepper salsa (such as Jardine's)
¼   teaspoon salt
4   (8-inch) fat-free flour tortillas
¼   cup sliced green onions
¼   cup low-fat sour cream
¼   cup (1 ounce) shredded reduced-fat Monterey Jack cheese

1. Place tofu in a shallow dish. Sprinkle with cumin, chili powder, vinegar, and cinnamon; toss gently to coat. Set aside.

2. Heat oil in a large nonstick skillet over medium heat. Add onion, and sauté 2 minutes. Add bell pepper and zucchini, and sauté 4 minutes. Stir in tofu mixture, salsa, and salt, and cook 2 minutes, stirring occasionally. Remove from heat.

3. Warm the flour tortillas according to package directions. Spoon about ¾ cup tofu mixture down center of each tortilla. Top with 1 tablespoon each of green onions, sour cream, and cheese; roll up tortillas. Yield: 4 servings (serving size: 1 burrito).

Note: Tofu, which has a nondescript taste on its own, acts like a dry sponge, soaking up the flavor of whatever it is cooked with. In this recipe, it absorbs the flavors of the seasonings—cumin, chili powder, and cinnamon.

POINTS: 5; **Exchanges:** 2 Starch, 1 Veg, ½ Med-fat Meat, ½ Fat
Per serving: CAL 231 (26% from fat); PRO 10.1g; FAT 6.7g (sat 2.4g); CARB 31.8g; FIB 1.6g; CHOL 10mg; IRON 1.2mg; SOD 794mg; CALC 99mg

Mediterranean Lentil Bake

2   (14½-ounce) cans one-third-less salt chicken broth
1   cup uncooked basmati rice
¾   cup lentils
¾   cup chopped green onions
½   cup (2 ounces) crumbled feta cheese with basil and tomato
1   teaspoon dried oregano
¼   teaspoon Greek seasoning
1   garlic clove, minced
Cooking spray

1. Preheat oven to 350°.

2. Combine first 8 ingredients in a 2-quart casserole coated with cooking spray. Cover and bake at 350° for 1½ hours or until lentils are tender. Yield: 6 servings (serving size: 1 cup).

POINTS: 4; **Exchanges:** 2½ Starch, 1 Very Lean Meat
Per serving: CAL 236 (10% from fat); PRO 12.8g; FAT 2.6g (sat 1.4g); CARB 40.5g; FIB 3.4g; CHOL 7mg; IRON 3.8mg; SOD 550mg; CALC 68mg

Spaghetti With Lentil-Mushroom Sauce

Olive oil-flavored cooking spray
1   teaspoon olive oil
1   cup chopped green onions
¾   cup diced carrot
4   garlic cloves, minced
1   (8-ounce) package presliced mushrooms, coarsely chopped
2½ cups water
1¼ cups lentils
¼   teaspoon crushed red pepper
¼   teaspoon black pepper
1   (10½-ounce) can beef consommé
1   (26-ounce) jar low-fat sun-dried tomato and herb pasta sauce
8   cups hot cooked thin spaghetti (about 16 ounces uncooked pasta)
½   cup (2 ounces) shredded fresh Parmesan cheese

1. Coat a Dutch oven with cooking spray; add oil, and place over medium-high heat until hot. Add green onions, carrot, and garlic; sauté until crisp-tender. Add mushrooms; sauté 3 minutes or until tender. Stir in water, lentils, crushed red pepper, black pepper, and beef consommé; bring

Unlike most beans, lentils do not have to be soaked before cooking—but they should be thoroughly rinsed—and they cook faster than other dried beans. One cup will yield 2 cups of cooked lentils. Drain lentils as soon as they're done or they will continue to cook. A half-cup of cooked lentils is an excellent source of folic acid, is a good source of vegetable protein, is virtually fat-free, and contains just 100 calories. It also provides 4 grams of dietary fiber and plenty of complex carbohydrates.

CHICKPEAS (GARBANZO BEANS)

Chickpeas are a good source of protein, calcium, iron, and B vitamins. They are available canned, dried, and—in some areas—fresh. One cup of dried chickpeas yields about 3 cups cooked. Chickpeas are used in salads, soups, and stews, but are perhaps best known as the main ingredient in hummus, a Middle Eastern purée.

to a boil. Cover, reduce heat, and simmer 35 minutes. Add pasta sauce; cook an additional 10 minutes. Spoon sauce over pasta; top with cheese. Yield: 8 servings (serving size: 1 cup spaghetti, 1 cup sauce, and 1 tablespoon cheese).

POINTS: 7; **Exchanges:** 4½ Starch, 1 Very Lean Meat, 1 Veg
Per serving: CAL 420 (10% from fat); PRO 23.1g; FAT 4.5g (sat 1.6g); CARB 73g; FIB 8.1g; CHOL 6mg; IRON 6.6mg; SOD 695mg; CALC 199mg

Roasted Curried Vegetables With Garbanzo Beans

For variety, try these roasted vegetables with a dollop of plain fat-free yogurt. The tart flavor and creamy texture of yogurt works well with the aromatic seasonings in this dish.

2   cups diagonally sliced carrot
2   cups cubed red bell pepper
2   medium yellow onions, each cut into 8 wedges
1   (19-ounce) can chickpeas (garbanzo beans), drained
3   tablespoons rice wine vinegar
1   tablespoon olive oil
1   teaspoon curry powder
1   teaspoon peeled minced fresh ginger
¼   teaspoon salt
Cooking spray

1. Preheat oven to 450°.
2. Combine first 9 ingredients in a large bowl; toss gently to coat.
3. Place mixture on a jelly-roll pan coated with cooking spray. Bake at 450° for 28 minutes or until vegetables are lightly browned, stirring once. Yield: 7 servings (serving size: 1 cup).

POINTS: 2; **Exchanges:** 1 Starch, 1 Veg, ½ Fat
Per serving: CAL 137 (23% from fat); PRO 5.4g; FAT 3.5g (sat 0.5g); CARB 22.3g; FIB 4.2g; CHOL 0mg; IRON 2.2mg; SOD 194mg; CALC 44mg

Marinated Black-eyed Pea Salad

Cooking spray
1   cup chopped onion
3   cups shelled black-eyed peas (about 1 pound unshelled)
2¼ cups water
¼   cup chopped cooked ham
¼   teaspoon pepper
1   (10½-ounce) can low-salt chicken broth
2   tablespoons white wine vinegar
1   tablespoon olive oil
1   tablespoon lemon juice
1   teaspoon honey
½   teaspoon salt
½   teaspoon dried dill
½   teaspoon dried thyme
¼   teaspoon pepper
2   garlic cloves, crushed
1   cup halved cherry tomatoes
⅓   cup sliced green onions
Fresh spinach leaves (optional)

1. Coat a saucepan with cooking spray; place over medium heat. Add onion; sauté 5 minutes. Stir in peas and next 4 ingredients; bring to a boil. Cover, reduce heat, and simmer 30 minutes, stirring occasionally. Drain; set aside.
2. Combine vinegar and next 8 ingredients in a large bowl; stir well with a whisk. Add pea mixture, tomatoes, and green onions; toss gently. Cover and marinate in refrigerator 8 hours. Spoon into a spinach-lined bowl, if desired. Yield: 8 servings (serving size: 1 cup).

POINTS: 2; **Exchanges:** 1 Starch, ½ Fat, ½ Very Lean Meat
Per serving: CAL 124 (27% from fat); PRO 7.4g; FAT 3.7g (sat 0.8g); CARB 16.8g; FIB 1.9g; CHOL 4mg; IRON 1.2mg; SOD 256mg; CALC 29mg

Marinated Black-eyed Pea Salad

Chunky Beef-and-Vegetable Chili

¾ pound ground chuck
2 cups sliced fresh mushrooms
1 cup chopped onion
1 cup diced yellow bell pepper
3 garlic cloves, crushed
2½ cups diced zucchini
1½ cups water
1 cup diced carrot
2½ tablespoons chili powder
1 tablespoon sugar
2½ teaspoons ground cumin
1½ teaspoons dried oregano
½ teaspoon salt
¼ teaspoon pepper
¼ teaspoon hot sauce
2 (16-ounce) cans kidney beans, drained
2 (14.5-ounce) cans no-salt-added whole tomatoes, undrained and coarsely chopped
2 (8-ounce) cans no-salt-added tomato sauce

1. Cook first 5 ingredients in a large Dutch oven over medium-high heat until beef is browned, stirring to crumble beef. Drain well; return beef mixture to pan. Add remaining ingredients; bring to a boil. Partially cover, reduce heat, and simmer 1½ hours or until thick, stirring occasionally. Yield: 8 servings (serving size: 1½ cups).

POINTS: 5; **Exchanges:** 2 Starch, 1 Veg, 1 Med-fat Meat
Per serving: CAL 256 (24% from fat); PRO 16.8g; FAT 6.9g (sat 2.5g); CARB 34.2g; FIB 4.9g; CHOL 25mg; IRON 4.6mg; SOD 356mg; CALC 92mg

Barbecued Meat Loaf

1 cup drained canned pinto beans
½ cup finely chopped onion
⅓ cup finely chopped green bell pepper
¼ cup dry breadcrumbs
2 teaspoons low-salt Worcestershire sauce
¼ teaspoon salt
¼ teaspoon pepper
⅛ teaspoon hot sauce
2 garlic cloves, minced
1 large egg white, lightly beaten
⅓ cup barbecue sauce, divided
¾ pound ground round
½ pound lean ground pork
Cooking spray

1. Preheat oven to 350°.

2. Combine first 10 ingredients in a large bowl; stir in 1 tablespoon barbecue sauce. Crumble ground round and ground pork into bowl, stirring just until blended.

3. Shape mixture into an 8½- x 4-inch loaf on a broiler pan coated with cooking spray. Brush 2 tablespoons barbecue sauce over meat loaf.

4. Bake at 350° for 1 hour. Brush remaining barbecue sauce over meat loaf. Bake an additional 10 minutes or until done. Let stand 5 minutes before slicing. Yield: 8 servings.

POINTS: 3; **Exchanges:** 2½ Lean Meat, ½ Starch
Per serving: CAL 168 (24% from fat); PRO 18.9g; FAT 4.5g (sat 1.5g); CARB 11.9g; FIB 1.5g; CHOL 43mg; IRON 2.5mg; SOD 297mg; CALC 25mg

Lima Bean-Sweet Potato Bake

1¼ cups dried baby lima beans (about ½ [16-ounce] package)
6 cups water
1 cup coarsely chopped onion
3 cups (½-inch) peeled cubed sweet potato
½ cup chopped green bell pepper
2 bacon slices, cooked and crumbled
1 cup water
½ cup ketchup
¼ cup honey
2 tablespoons brown sugar

Serve Chunky Beef-and-Vegetable Chili with coleslaw and corn muffins.

1 teaspoon grated orange rind
½ teaspoon salt
¼ teaspoon ground cumin
Cooking spray

1. Sort and wash beans; place in a large saucepan. Cover with water to 2 inches above beans. Bring to a boil, and cook 2 minutes. Remove from heat; cover and let stand 1 hour. Drain.

2. Return beans to pan. Add 6 cups water and onion; bring to a boil. Cover, reduce heat, and simmer 45 minutes or just until beans are tender. Drain well. Cook sweet potato in boiling water 10 minutes; drain well.

3. Preheat oven to 325°.

4. Combine sweet potato, beans, green pepper, and bacon in a bowl; toss gently. Combine 1 cup water, ketchup, and next 5 ingredients; pour over sweet potato mixture, and toss gently to coat. Spoon mixture into a 2-quart casserole coated with cooking spray. Bake at 325° for 1½ hours.

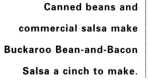

Canned beans and commercial salsa make Buckaroo Bean-and-Bacon Salsa a cinch to make.

Remove from oven; let stand 10 minutes before serving. Yield: 6 servings (serving size: 1 cup).

Note: You may substitute 3 cups frozen baby lima beans for the dried limas, if desired. Cook beans according to package directions, omitting salt; drain. Cook onion with sweet potato. Combine beans, sweet potato mixture, green pepper, and bacon; proceed as directed in recipe.

POINTS: 5; **Exchanges:** 4 Starch
Per serving: CAL 292 (6% from fat); PRO 10.1g; FAT 2g (sat 0.6g); CARB 60.9g; FIB 7g; CHOL 2mg; IRON 3.2mg; SOD 485mg; CALC 58mg

Buckaroo Bean-and-Bacon Salsa

Cooking spray
1 cup chopped onion
2 garlic cloves, minced
1 (15-ounce) can black-eyed peas, rinsed and drained
1 (15-ounce) can black beans, rinsed and drained
1 (15-ounce) can pinquito or pinto beans, rinsed and drained

1   (14.5-ounce) jar salsa with chipotle chiles
1   (14.5-ounce) jar salsa with cilantro
4   bacon slices, cooked, drained, and crumbled
2   tablespoons chopped fresh cilantro

1. Coat a large nonstick skillet with cooking spray; place over medium heat until hot. Add onion; sauté 5 minutes or until tender. Add garlic; sauté 1 minute. Add peas, beans, salsas, and bacon; cover and cook until thoroughly heated. Remove from heat; stir in cilantro. Serve warm with baked tortilla chips. Yield: 14 servings (serving size: ½ cup).

POINTS: 1; **Exchanges:** 1 Starch
Per serving: CAL 91 (7% from fat); PRO 5.4g; FAT 0.7g (sat 0.2g); CARB 17.1g; FIB 3.3g; CHOL 1mg; IRON 2mg; SOD 301mg; CALC 23mg

Red Bean Spice Cake

1   cup drained canned red beans
1¼ cups sugar, divided
Cooking spray
2   cups plus 1 tablespoon self-rising flour, divided
½   cup vegetable oil
½   teaspoon ground cinnamon
¼   teaspoon ground ginger
¼   teaspoon ground nutmeg
¼   teaspoon ground cloves
1   large egg
2   large egg whites
1   (4-ounce) jar plums with apples baby food
1   cup sifted powdered sugar
1½ tablespoons lemon juice
2   tablespoons finely chopped pecans, toasted

1. Preheat oven to 350°.

2. Combine beans and ¼ cup sugar in a bowl; mash well with a potato masher.

3. Coat a 10-inch Bundt pan with cooking spray; dust with 1 tablespoon flour.

4. Combine bean mixture, remaining 1 cup sugar, remaining 2 cups flour, vegetable oil, and next 7 ingredients in a large bowl; beat at low speed of a mixer until smooth. Pour batter into prepared pan.

5. Bake at 350° for 45 minutes or until a wooden pick inserted in center comes out clean. Let cool in pan 15 minutes on a wire rack; remove from pan. Let cool completely on wire rack.

6. Combine powdered sugar and lemon juice, stirring until smooth. Drizzle icing over cake; sprinkle with pecans. Yield: 16 servings.

POINTS: 5; **Exchanges:** 2 Starch, ½ Fruit, 1 Fat
Per serving: CAL 238 (30% from fat); PRO 3.2g; FAT 8g (sat 1.4g); CARB 38.7g; FIB 1.5g; CHOL 13mg; IRON 1mg; SOD 268mg; CALC 61mg

Black Bean Cakes With Pineapple Salsa

2   (15-ounce) cans black beans, undrained
½   cup sliced green onions
2   tablespoons fresh lime juice
1   teaspoon ground cumin
½   teaspoon dried oregano
2   garlic cloves, minced
1   cup (2 ounces) finely crushed salsa and cream cheese-flavored baked tortilla chips
½   cup (2 ounces) shredded Monterey Jack cheese with jalapeño peppers
Cooking spray
Pineapple Salsa

1. Drain beans, reserving ½ cup liquid. Place beans and reserved liquid in a large bowl. Stir in green onions, lime juice, cumin, oregano, and garlic. Place 1 cup bean mixture in a food processor, and process until smooth. Stir puréed bean mixture into remaining bean mixture. Stir in crushed chips and cheese, and let stand 5 minutes or until thick.

2. Spoon ⅓ cup bean mixture for each patty onto a sheet of wax paper; shape each portion into a 3-inch cake. Coat a nonstick skillet with cooking spray; place over medium-high heat until hot. Add 4 to 6 cakes; cook 1½ minutes on each side or until browned. Remove from skillet; set aside, and keep warm. Repeat procedure with remaining cakes. Serve with Pineapple Salsa. Yield: 6 servings (serving size: 2 cakes and ½ cup salsa).

POINTS: 4; **Exchanges:** 2 Starch, ½ Fruit, 1 Very Lean Meat, ½ Fat
Per serving: CAL 255 (19% from fat); PRO 11.8g; FAT 5.4g (sat 2g); CARB 39g; FIB 9.7g; CHOL 7mg; IRON 4mg; SOD 585mg; CALC 153mg

Sometimes called turtle beans, black beans have a shiny exterior and rich-tasting meat. Because of their slightly tangy flavor, black beans fare well paired with acidic ingredients, smoked meats, cilantro, onions, and tomatoes. Of course, they also make a wonderful soup. Their protein content is 23% with lots of iron, calcium, and B vitamins. Black beans are available canned and dried: One cup dried black beans yields 2 to 2½ cups cooked beans.

TOFU

Tofu is made from soy milk, which is iron-rich and has more protein than cow's milk. Look for tofu in Asian markets, health-food stores, and many super-markets. It is available vacuum-packed, in water, and in bulk. Firm and extra-firm tofu can be cubed and added to stir-fry; soft tofu can be whipped into dips, puddings, soups, and scrambled eggs.

Storage

If you purchase tofu packed in water, drain it, cover with fresh water, and refrigerate for no more than a week. Change the water every day. You can freeze tofu, without water, for up to three months (but be forewarned: It will have a somewhat chewier texture when thawed). Vacuum-packed tofu doesn't need to be refrigerated until it is opened.

Pineapple Salsa:

1   (20-ounce) can unsweetened pineapple tidbits, drained
½   cup finely chopped red bell pepper
½   cup finely chopped green bell pepper
2   tablespoons chopped fresh cilantro
1   tablespoon fresh lime juice
1   tablespoon seeded minced jalapeño pepper

1. Combine all ingredients in a bowl; toss well. Serve at room temperature. Yield: 3 cups.

Tortilla Pie

Serve this hearty meatless main dish topped with salsa and sour cream, if desired.

1   (15-ounce) can no-salt-added kidney beans, undrained
1   (1.25-ounce) package 40%-less-salt taco seasoning
Cooking spray
8   (8-inch) flour tortillas
1   cup chunky salsa, divided
Mock Guacamole
1   (8-ounce) package reduced-fat shredded Mexican blend cheese (such as Sargento)

1. Preheat oven to 350°.
2. Combine beans and taco seasoning; stir well. Partially mash beans with a fork; set aside.
3. Coat a 9-inch round cake pan with cooking spray; place 1 tortilla in bottom of pan. Spread half of bean mixture over tortilla; place 1 tortilla over bean mixture. Spread ½ cup salsa over tortilla; top with 1 tortilla. Spread half of Mock Guacamole over tortilla; top with 1 tortilla. Sprinkle with 1 cup cheese; top with 1 tortilla. Repeat layers with remaining ingredients except cheese. Cover with foil; bake at 350° for 45 minutes. Uncover; sprinkle with remaining cheese, and bake an additional 5 minutes or until cheese melts. Cut pie into 6 wedges. Yield: 6 servings.
Note: We found that a deep-sided cake pan works best for this recipe. Our test kitchens staff used a 3-inch-deep Wilton pan.

POINTS: 8; **Exchanges:** 4 Starch, 1½ Med-fat Meat
Per serving: CAL 426 (27% from fat); PRO 22.5g; FAT 12.8g (sat 5.6g); CARB 58.1g; FIB 8.9g; CHOL 15mg; IRON 3.9mg; SOD 1118mg; CALC 408mg

---

Mock Guacamole:

1   (10-ounce) package frozen baby lima beans
1   tablespoon chopped fresh cilantro
2   tablespoons minced fresh onion
2   tablespoons light mayonnaise
2   tablespoons lime juice
1   tablespoon water
¼   teaspoon ground cumin
¼   teaspoon chili powder
⅛   teaspoon hot sauce
2   garlic cloves, minced

1. Cook lima beans in boiling water 16 minutes or until very tender; drain.
2. Place beans, cilantro, and remaining ingredients in a food processor; process until smooth, scraping sides of processor bowl occasionally. Yield: 1¾ cups.

Thai-Seared Tofu

½   cup chopped fresh basil
½   cup chopped fresh cilantro
½   cup low-salt soy sauce
½   cup fresh lime juice
¼   cup chopped fresh mint
2   tablespoons molasses
1   tablespoon peeled minced fresh ginger
1   tablespoon vegetable oil
2   teaspoons curry powder
½   teaspoon crushed red pepper
4   garlic cloves, minced
2   (10.5-ounce) packages reduced-fat firm tofu, drained
Cooking spray
6   cups hot cooked vermicelli (about 12 ounces uncooked pasta)

1. Combine first 11 ingredients in a large baking dish; stir with a whisk until blended. Cut each tofu cake crosswise into 4 slices. Place tofu slices in soy sauce mixture, turning to coat slices. Cover and marinate in refrigerator at least 2 hours.
2. Remove tofu slices from dish, reserving marinade. Coat a large nonstick skillet with cooking spray; place over medium-high heat. Add tofu slices; cook 2 minutes on each side. Remove from skillet; set aside, and keep warm.
3. Add reserved marinade to skillet; bring to a

simmer. Spoon noodles onto individual plates; top with tofu slices. Drizzle marinade over tofu and noodles. Yield: 4 servings (serving size: 1½ cups noodles, 2 tofu slices, and ½ cup sauce).

POINTS: 9; Exchanges: 5 Starch, ½ Med-fat Meat
Per serving: CAL 450 (14% from fat); PRO 19.7g; FAT 7.1g (sat 1.1g); CARB 73.6g; FIB 4.2g; CHOL 0mg; IRON 4.3mg; SOD 914mg; CALC 68mg

White Bean-and-Tofu-Stuffed Shells

Boil extra pasta shells in case a few tear during cooking or stuffing.

2   tablespoons sun-dried tomatoes, packed without oil
2   (10.5-ounce) packages firm tofu
2   (15-ounce) cans cannellini or other white beans, rinsed and drained
1   cup (4 ounces) shredded part-skim mozzarella cheese
1   tablespoon chopped fresh or 1 teaspoon dried basil
1   teaspoon dried Italian seasoning
½   teaspoon crushed red pepper
2   garlic cloves, minced
2   cups low-salt pasta sauce
Cooking spray
18 cooked jumbo pasta shells
½   cup (2 ounces) shredded part-skim mozzarella cheese
2   tablespoons grated Parmesan cheese
Fresh basil (optional)

1. Preheat oven to 375°.

2. Place sun-dried tomatoes in a small bowl, and cover with hot water. Cover and let stand 10 minutes. Drain well, and chop.

3. Place tofu in a food processor, and process until smooth. Spoon tofu onto several layers of heavy-duty paper towels, and spread to ½-inch thickness. Cover with additional paper towels, and let stand 5 minutes.

4. Scrape puréed tofu into food processor using

The marinade for Thai-Seared Tofu doubles as a sauce.

Full of meat and vegetables, Kentucky Burgoo is popular for large Southern gatherings.

a rubber spatula. Add chopped sun-dried tomatoes, beans, mozzarella cheese, basil, Italian seasoning, pepper, and garlic; pulse until beans are coarsely chopped.

5. Spread 1 cup of pasta sauce on bottom of a 13-x 9-inch baking dish coated with cooking spray. Spoon ¼ cup tofu mixture into each pasta shell, and arrange shells in baking dish. Spoon remaining pasta sauce over shells, and sprinkle ½ cup mozzarella cheese and Parmesan cheese evenly over shells.

6. Bake at 375° for 30 minutes or until mozzarella cheese begins to brown. Garnish with fresh basil, if desired. Yield: 7 servings (serving size: 2 shells).

POINTS: 9; **Exchanges:** 4 Starch, 1½ Med-fat Meat, 1 Veg
Per serving: CAL 444 (19% from fat); PRO 24.1g; FAT 9.4g (sat 2.9g); CARB 65.5g; FIB 3.8g; CHOL 12mg; IRON 5.6mg; SOD 162mg; CALC 245mg

Kentucky Burgoo

1   pound lean boned chuck steak
1½ teaspoons vegetable oil
8   cups fat-free beef broth
1   pound skinned, boned chicken thighs
4   cups peeled cubed baking potato (about 1½ pounds)
2½ cups chopped carrot
1   cup chopped celery
1   cup chopped onion
1½ teaspoons curry powder
1   teaspoon dried thyme
½   teaspoon salt
1   (14.5-ounce) can diced tomatoes, undrained
1   garlic clove, minced
2   cups frozen whole-kernel corn, thawed
1   (10-ounce) package frozen lima beans, thawed

1. Trim fat from steak; cut steak into 1-inch cubes. Heat oil in a large Dutch oven over medium-high heat. Add steak; brown well on all sides. Add broth; bring to a boil. Cover, reduce heat, and simmer 1 hour.

2. Trim fat from chicken thighs; cut chicken into 1-inch cubes. Add chicken, potato, and next 8 ingredients to pan; simmer, uncovered, 30 minutes or until vegetables are tender. Add corn and lima beans to stew; cook an additional 15 minutes or until beans are tender. Yield: 10 servings (serving size: 1½ cups).

POINTS: 5; **Exchanges:** 2 Starch, 2 Lean Meat
Per serving: CAL 257 (20% from fat); PRO 18.2g; FAT 5.7g (sat 1.8g); CARB 32.4g; FIB 4.1g; CHOL 24mg; IRON 3.2mg; SOD 308mg; CALC 54mg

Rosemary Focaccia

1 (16-ounce) can navy beans, rinsed and drained
3½ cups all-purpose flour
1½ tablespoons chopped fresh rosemary
1 teaspoon kosher salt, divided
4 teaspoons olive oil, divided
1 package rapid rise yeast
1 cup very warm water (120° to 130°)
Olive oil-flavored cooking spray

1. Attach dough hook to a heavy-duty mixer. Place beans in a large mixing bowl, and mash with a potato masher. Stir in flour, rosemary, ½ teaspoon salt, 2 teaspoons oil, and yeast. Add very warm water, and beat with dough hook at medium speed until dough is smooth and elastic (about 5 minutes).

2. Press dough into a 15- x 10-inch jelly-roll pan coated with cooking spray. Using the handle of a wooden spoon or your fingertips, make indentations in top of dough. Gently brush dough with remaining 2 teaspoons oil, and sprinkle with remaining ½ teaspoon salt. Let rise in a warm place (85°), free from drafts, 30 minutes or until doubled in bulk.

3. Preheat oven to 400°.

4. Bake at 400° for 20 minutes or until lightly browned. Cut into squares. Yield: 18 servings.

POINTS: 2; **Exchanges:** 1½ Starch
Per serving: CAL 105 (11% from fat); PRO 3.7g; FAT 1.3g (sat 0.2g); CARB 20g; FIB 1.1g; CHOL 0mg; IRON 1.3mg; SOD 170mg; CALC 11mg

Honey-Roasted Soybean Snack Mix

Look for dried soybeans at your local health-food store.

1 cup dried soybeans
Cooking spray
3 cups multi-grain toasted O-shaped cereal (such as Multi-Grain Cheerios)
3 cups crisscross of corn and rice cereal (such as Crispix)
3 cups fat-free tiny pretzel twists
¼ cup honey
¼ cup light-colored corn syrup
2 tablespoons reduced-calorie stick margarine, melted
¼ teaspoon salt

1. Sort and wash beans; place in a medium bowl. Cover with water to 2 inches above beans; let stand 8 hours. Drain in a colander, pressing with paper towels until barely moist.

2. Preheat oven to 350°.

3. Place soybeans in a large roasting pan coated with cooking spray. Bake at 350° for 15 minutes; stir well. Bake an additional 25 minutes or until beans are lightly browned, stirring every 5 minutes. Reduce oven temperature to 300°.

4. Stir cereals and pretzels into soybeans. Combine honey, corn syrup, melted margarine, and salt; pour over cereal mixture, stirring well to coat. Bake at 300° for 45 minutes, stirring after 15 minutes.

5. Spoon snack mix onto a large sheet of wax paper, and let cool completely. Store in an airtight container for up to 2 weeks. Yield: 20 servings (serving size: ½ cup).

Note: Don't use quick-soak method or soak soybeans more than 8 hours or they will become soft and chewy and will never get crisp during baking. We found that using an 18- x 12-inch roasting pan with deep sides worked best for stirring cereal mixture in oven. If you don't have a large roasting pan, 2 (13- x 9-inch) baking pans may be used.

POINTS: 2; **Exchanges:** 1½ Starch
Per serving: CAL 113 (20% from fat); PRO 4.2g; FAT 2.5g (sat 0.3g); CARB 20.1g; FIB 2.8g; CHOL 0mg; IRON 4.3mg; SOD 170mg; CALC 35mg

SOYBEANS

Studies show that substituting soy for animal protein (such as meat) lowers "bad" cholesterol and may reduce the risk of cancer and arterial clots. Because soy contains isoflavones, which act like estrogen, it may also alleviate the symptoms of menopause.

Soybeans can be found at most supermarkets and health-food stores. Most canned soybeans are yellow, but brown and black varieties are also available. One cup dried beans yields 3 cups cooked. Once soaked, they can be cooked like any other dried bean to be used in soups, stews, and more.

Almighty Ingredients

Old wives' tales aside, these foods are magic.

How else could such small amounts lend a dish so much flavor?

While some old wives' tales sound remarkably close to the truth, others are outlandishly silly. So in the end, we discount anything that smacks of superstition. In general, a little skepticism is a good thing. Eating yogurt, for instance, doesn't ensure longevity, and eating almonds before drinking won't reduce your chances of having a hangover. But when it comes to nutrition, there's a big difference between skepticism and closed mindedness. Drinking tea does, after all, seem to lower the risk of cancer. And although the effectiveness of the groom wearing garlic in his buttonhole to ensure a successful wedding night has never been studied, some scientific evidence does suggest that garlic lowers cholesterol and prevents heart disease. Regardless of their medical powers, ginger, garlic, honey, and other almighty ingredients have at least one proven ability: They impart incredible flavor to any dish. Once you've tasted Roasted Garlic Pesto Pizza and Earl Grey Sorbet, you'll agree that the health benefits of these foods are just an added bonus. And if you ever figure out whether sprinkling chili powder in your ski boots really does keep your feet warm, let us know.

Fat-free sweetened condensed milk gives Almond Crème Caramel a rich texture.

4. Remove cake pan from water, and place on a wire rack. Remove foil. Let custard cool in pan 30 minutes. Loosen edges with a knife or rubber spatula. Place a serving plate upside down on top of cake pan, and invert custard onto plate, allowing syrup to drizzle over custard. Sprinkle with additional toasted sliced almonds, if desired. Yield: 9 servings.

POINTS: 5; **Exchanges:** ½ Sk Milk, 2½ Starch
Per serving: CAL 253 (15% from fat); PRO 9.8g; FAT 4.3g (sat 0.9g); CARB 43.1g; FIB 0.4g; CHOL 100mg; IRON 0.6mg; SOD 118mg; CALC 131mg

Chile Con Queso Dip

1   (14.5-ounce) can diced tomatoes, undrained
1   (10-ounce) can diced tomatoes with green chiles, undrained
1   teaspoon olive oil
½   cup chopped onion
2   garlic cloves, minced
1   (8-ounce) block fat-free cream cheese, softened
1   teaspoon chili powder
6   ounces light processed cheese, cubed (such as Velveeta Light)
Cilantro sprigs (optional)

1. Drain diced tomatoes and diced tomatoes with green chiles in a colander over a medium bowl, reserving ⅓ cup liquid; set tomatoes and reserved liquid aside.

2. Heat olive oil in a medium saucepan over medium heat. Add chopped onion and minced garlic, and sauté 4 minutes. Add softened cream cheese, and cook until cheese melts, stirring constantly. Add tomatoes, reserved liquid, and chili powder; bring mixture to a boil. Add processed cheese; reduce heat, and simmer 3 minutes or until cheese melts, stirring constantly. Garnish with cilantro sprigs, if desired. Serve dip warm with baked tortilla chips. Yield: 14 servings (serving size: ¼ cup).

POINTS: 1; **Exchanges:** ½ Starch, ½ Lean Meat
Per serving: CAL 63 (24% from fat); PRO 5.5g; FAT 1.7g (sat 0.9g); CARB 6.4g; FIB 0.3g; CHOL 7mg; IRON 0.3mg; SOD 400mg; CALC 132mg

This Chile Con Queso Dip is a lightened version of the popular Tex-Mex appetizer.

Almond Crème Caramel

½   cup sugar
4   large eggs
1   teaspoon vanilla extract
½   teaspoon almond extract
1   (14-ounce) can fat-free sweetened condensed milk
1   (12-ounce) can evaporated skim milk
¼   cup coarsely chopped sliced almonds
Sliced almonds, toasted (optional)

1. Preheat oven to 350°.

2. Pour sugar into a 9-inch round cake pan. Place cake pan over medium heat; cook 6 minutes or until sugar is dissolved and golden, shaking cake pan occasionally with tongs. Immediately remove from heat; set aside.

3. Place eggs in a bowl; stir with a whisk until foamy. Add extracts and milks; stir with a whisk. Pour mixture into prepared cake pan; sprinkle chopped almonds over egg mixture. Cover with foil; place in a large shallow roasting pan. Place roasting pan in oven; add water to pan to a depth of 1-inch. Bake at 350° for 55 minutes or until a knife inserted in center comes out clean.

Tea-and-Currant Loaf

1½ cups strong brewed tea
1 cup firmly packed dark brown sugar
¾ cup dried currants
⅓ cup golden raisins
⅓ cup raisins
¼ cup candied orange peel
2 teaspoons rum extract
2 tablespoons stick margarine, melted
1 large egg, lightly beaten
2 cups all-purpose flour
1½ teaspoons baking powder
2 teaspoons grated lemon rind
½ teaspoon ground cinnamon
¼ teaspoon salt
¼ teaspoon ground nutmeg
¼ teaspoon ground mace
Cooking spray

1. Combine first 7 ingredients; stir well. Cover and let stand 8 hours. Stir in margarine and egg.

2. Preheat oven to 350°.

3. Combine flour and next 6 ingredients; make a well in center of mixture. Add tea mixture to flour mixture, stirring until moist. Divide batter between 2 (7½- x 3¾-inch) loaf pans coated with cooking spray. Bake at 350° for 50 minutes. Let cool in pans 10 minutes; remove from pans, and let cool completely on wire rack. Yield: 2 loaves, 8 servings per loaf (serving size: 1 slice).

POINTS: 3; **Exchanges:** 1½ Starch, 1 Fruit
Per serving: CAL 173 (11% from fat); PRO 2.5g; FAT 2.2g (sat 0.4g); CARB 36.6g; FIB 0.9g; CHOL 14mg; IRON 1.7mg; SOD 68mg; CALC 56mg

Chicken With Pecan-Parsley Cream

3 tablespoons all-purpose flour
½ teaspoon freshly ground pepper
¼ teaspoon salt
4 (4-ounce) skinned, boned chicken breast halves
2 teaspoons olive oil
¼ cup finely chopped pecans
1 cup low-salt chicken broth
⅓ cup grated Parmesan cheese
⅓ cup sweet Marsala
4 ounces block-style fat-free cream cheese, cubed
⅓ cup finely chopped fresh parsley

1 garlic clove, minced
3 cups hot cooked instant rice
2 tablespoons grated Parmesan cheese
¼ cup pecan pieces
Parsley sprigs (optional)

1. Combine first 3 ingredients; stir well. Dredge chicken in flour mixture. Heat 2 teaspoons oil in a nonstick skillet over medium-high heat. Add chicken; cook 4 minutes on each side. Remove chicken; keep warm. Add pecans to skillet, and cook 3 minutes, stirring frequently. Add chicken broth, ⅓ cup Parmesan cheese, wine, and cream cheese, stirring until cream cheese melts. Remove from heat; stir in chopped parsley and garlic.

2. Spoon ¾ cup rice onto each of 4 plates; drizzle each with 3 tablespoons sauce. Top each with a chicken breast half; spoon 3 tablespoons sauce over chicken. Sprinkle each with 1½ teaspoons Parmesan cheese and 1 tablespoon pecan pieces. Garnish with parsley. Yield: 4 servings.

POINTS: 12; **Exchanges:** 4½ Very Lean Meat, 3 Starch, 3 Fat
Per serving: CAL 533 (28% from fat); PRO 40.9g; FAT 16.6g (sat 3.9g); CARB 47.1g; FIB 1.9g; CHOL 81mg; IRON 3.6mg; SOD 656mg; CALC 303mg

Strawberry Yogurt Frappé

3 cups fresh strawberries
1½ cups vanilla low-fat yogurt
1 cup orange juice
1 tablespoon honey
1 banana, peeled and quartered
10 tablespoons frozen reduced-calorie whipped topping, thawed
10 teaspoons slivered almonds, toasted

1. Remove green caps from strawberries; spread berries on a baking sheet and freeze. Place frozen strawberries, yogurt, and next 3 ingredients in a blender; process until smooth. Pour into glasses; top with whipped topping and almonds. Serve immediately. Yield: 5 servings (serving size: 1 cup frappé, 2 tablespoons whipped topping, and 2 teaspoons almonds).

POINTS: 3; **Exchanges:** 1 Fruit, 1 Starch, 1 Fat
Per serving: CAL 183 (22% from fat); PRO 5.5g; FAT 4.5g (sat 1g); CARB 32.8g; FIB 3.6g; CHOL 4mg; IRON 0.7mg; SOD 53mg; CALC 151mg

PEPERS

Bell peppers, which are sweet and mild, are low in calories and nutritionally dense. By weight, green bell peppers have twice the vitamin C as oranges; hot chiles have nearly 14 times as much. Hot chiles clear congestion, prevent blood clots, and temporarily raise your calorie-burning rate.

Shopping
Look for peppers with rich color; avoid those with soft spots or wrinkles. Generally, the smaller the pepper, the hotter it is. This is because small peppers have a higher percentage of seeds and veins, which contain up to 80% of the capsaicin, the chemical that makes chiles burn.

Storage
Peppers can be stored in a plastic bag in the refrigerator for up to two weeks.

PUMPKINSEED KERNELS

Pumpkinseed kernels are the richest plant source of zinc, which is vital to your immune system and sense of taste. There is evidence that they alleviate the symptoms of an enlarged prostate and help prevent bladder stones. While there are 11.4 grams of fat in a 1-ounce serving, 78% of the fat is unsaturated.

Shopping

Look for pumpkinseed kernels at health-food stores, Mexican markets, and some supermarkets. Available raw, roasted, and salted, they add savory flavor and crunchy texture to muffins, breads, and cakes.

Storage

You can store pumpkinseeds in an airtight container in the freezer for up to one year.

Pumpkinseed Quinoa Pilaf

Rinsing quinoa before cooking removes saponin, a naturally occurring soaplike substance on the outside of the grain. If you don't have a sieve fine enough to restrain this tiny grain, use cheesecloth to line the sieve.

¾ cup uncooked quinoa
1½ cups water
2   teaspoons olive oil
1   cup peeled diced jicama
1   cup chopped red onion
1   cup frozen whole-kernel corn, thawed
½   cup chopped red bell pepper
½   cup chopped green bell pepper
2   teaspoons seeded minced jalapeño pepper
1   cup chopped tomato
½   cup sliced green onions
⅓   cup unsalted pumpkinseed kernels, toasted
2   tablespoons chopped fresh cilantro
3   tablespoons fresh lime juice
½   teaspoon salt
1   small jalapeño (optional)

1. Place quinoa in a fine sieve; rinse thoroughly under cold water. Combine quinoa and 1½ cups water in a medium saucepan; bring to a boil. Cover, reduce heat, and simmer 20 minutes or until liquid is absorbed. Remove from heat; fluff with a fork. Set aside.

2. Heat olive oil in a large nonstick skillet over medium heat. Add diced jicama and next 5 ingredients; sauté 5 minutes or until tender. Add quinoa, tomato, and next 5 ingredients; sauté 1 minute or until thoroughly heated. Garnish with small jalapeño, if desired. Yield: 5 servings (serving size: 1 cup).

Note: Pumpkinseed kernels can be found in specialty and health-food stores.

POINTS: 4; **Exchanges:** 2 Starch, 1½ Fat
Per serving: CAL 228 (31% from fat); PRO 8.7g; FAT 7.9g (sat 2.2g); CARB 33.3g; FIB 4.3g; CHOL 0mg; IRON 5.1mg; SOD 249mg; CALC 57mg

Asian Pear-Cabbage Salad

2   cups very thinly sliced green cabbage
1   cup cubed Asian pear or ripe pear
1   cup peeled cubed fresh mango or persimmon
¼   cup unsalted pumpkinseed kernels, toasted
6   tablespoons white vinegar
2   tablespoons low-salt soy sauce
4   teaspoons sugar
⅛   teaspoon garlic powder
Dash of salt

1. Place ½ cup cabbage on each of 4 plates; top each with ¼ cup pear and ¼ cup mango. Sprinkle pumpkinseeds evenly over salads. Combine remaining ingredients; stir well. Drizzle dressing evenly over salads. Yield: 4 servings.

POINTS: 2; **Exchanges:** 1½ Fruit, 1 Fat
Per serving: CAL 125 (31% from fat); PRO 3.2g; FAT 4.3g (sat 0.8g); CARB 21.6g; FIB 2.6g; CHOL 0mg; IRON 1.8mg; SOD 324mg; CALC 29mg

Peggy Sue's Honey-Cinnamon Date-Nut Cake

½   cup stick margarine, softened
½   cup sugar
½   cup firmly packed brown sugar
3   cups all-purpose flour
1   teaspoon baking soda
½   teaspoon salt
1½ teaspoons ground cinnamon
1   cup evaporated skim milk
1   cup honey
½   cup applesauce
1   cup chopped pitted dates
¼   cup chopped walnuts, toasted
Cooking spray

1. Preheat oven to 350°.

2. Beat margarine and sugars at medium speed of a mixer until well blended (about 5 minutes). Combine flour, and next 3 ingredients; set aside. Combine milk, honey, and applesauce. Add flour mixture to margarine mixture alternately with honey mixture, beginning and ending with flour mixture. Stir in dates and walnuts.

3. Pour batter into a 13- x 9-inch baking pan coated with cooking spray. Bake at 350° for 55 minutes or until a wooden pick inserted in center comes out clean. Cool in pan on a wire rack. Yield: 16 servings.

POINTS: 5; **Exchanges:** 1 Fat, 2 Starch, 1 Fruit
Per serving: CAL 248 (21% from fat); PRO 3.6g; FAT 5.7g (sat 1g); CARB 47.7g; FIB 1.5g; CHOL 1mg; IRON 1.3mg; SOD 193mg; CALC 53mg

Asian Pear-Cabbage Salad

Roasted Garlic Pesto Pizza

Roasted Garlic Pesto Pizza

2 whole garlic heads
1 cup fresh basil leaves
¼ cup water
1 tablespoon grated Romano cheese
1½ teaspoons lemon juice
⅛ teaspoon salt
⅛ teaspoon pepper
1 (10-ounce) package thin Italian
   cheese-flavored pizza crust (such
   as Boboli)
10 (¼-inch-thick) slices seeded tomato
¼ cup chopped fresh basil
¼ teaspoon salt
¼ teaspoon pepper
1 teaspoon extra-virgin olive oil
6 tablespoons (1½ ounces) finely shredded
   part-skim mozzarella cheese
⅓ cup grated Romano cheese

1. Preheat oven to 350°.

2. Remove white papery skin from garlic heads (do not peel or separate the cloves). Wrap each garlic head separately in foil. Bake at 350° for 1 hour, and let cool 10 minutes. Separate garlic cloves, and squeeze to extract garlic pulp. Discard the skins.

3. Increase oven temperature to 450°.

4. Place garlic pulp, fresh basil leaves, and next 5 ingredients in a food processor, and process until mixture is smooth, scraping sides of processor bowl once.

5. Spread basil mixture evenly over Italian cheese-flavored pizza crust, leaving a ½-inch border. Arrange tomato slices in a single layer over basil mixture. Sprinkle ¼ cup chopped basil, ¼ teaspoon salt, and ¼ teaspoon pepper over tomato slices, and drizzle with extra-virgin olive oil. Sprinkle shredded mozzarella cheese and ⅓ cup grated Romano cheese over pizza. Bake at 450° for 10 minutes or until cheese melts. Cut pizza into 10 slices. Yield: 5 servings (serving size: 2 slices).

POINTS: 6; **Exchanges:** 2 Starch, 1 Med-fat Meat,1 Veg
Per serving: CAL 274 (30% from fat); PRO 13g; FAT 9g (sat 4.1g); CARB 35.6g; FIB 1.5g; CHOL 14mg; IRON 1.4mg; SOD 642mg; CALC 353mg

Pear-Walnut Muffins

1½ cups all-purpose flour
⅔ cup firmly packed brown sugar
½ cup whole-wheat flour or all-purpose flour
1 tablespoon baking powder
½ teaspoon salt
½ teaspoon ground cinnamon
1¼ cups finely chopped pear
⅓ cup coarsely chopped walnuts, toasted
¾ cup 2% reduced-fat milk
2 tablespoons vegetable oil
1 large egg, lightly beaten
Cooking spray
1 tablespoon granulated sugar

1. Preheat oven to 400°.

2. Combine first 6 ingredients in a medium bowl; stir well. Stir in chopped pear and walnuts; make a well in center of mixture. Combine milk, oil, and egg in a bowl, and stir well. Add milk mixture to flour mixture, stirring just until moist (dough will be sticky).

3. Divide batter evenly among 12 muffin cups coated with cooking spray, and sprinkle with granulated sugar. Bake at 400° for 20 minutes or until a wooden pick inserted in center comes out clean. Remove muffins from pans immediately, and place on a wire rack. Yield: 1 dozen (serving size: 1 muffin).

POINTS: 4; **Exchanges:** 2 Starch, ½ Fat
Per serving: CAL 175 (27% from fat); PRO 4.3g; FAT 5.3g (sat 0.9g); CARB 28.6g; FIB 1.7g; CHOL 20mg; IRON 1.5mg; SOD 115mg; CALC 104mg

A sprinkling of sugar on top gives Pear-Walnut Muffins a sweet crust.

Herbed-Yogurt Tomatoes

4   large tomatoes
Cooking spray
½   cup plain fat-free yogurt
1   teaspoon all-purpose flour
1½ teaspoons chopped fresh marjoram or
      oregano
¼   teaspoon salt
¼   teaspoon ground pepper
¼   cup grated fresh Romano cheese

1. Preheat oven to 400°.

2. Cut a ½-inch slice from stem end of each tomato. Place, cut sides up, in an 8-inch square baking dish coated with cooking spray. Set aside.

3. Combine yogurt and next 4 ingredients; stir well. Spread 2 tablespoons yogurt mixture over tomatoes; sprinkle each with 1 tablespoon cheese. Bake at 400° for 30 minutes. Yield: 4 servings.

POINTS: 1; **Exchanges:** 1 Veg, ½ Med-fat Meat
Per serving: CAL 71 (30% from fat); PRO 4.9g; FAT 2.5g (sat 1.3g); CARB 8.2g; FIB 1.5g; CHOL 8mg; IRON 0.6mg; SOD 263mg; CALC 140mg

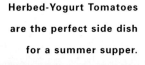

Herbed-Yogurt Tomatoes are the perfect side dish for a summer supper.

Maple-Black Walnut Muffins

Cooking spray
1¾ cups all-purpose flour
⅓   cup firmly packed brown sugar
¼   cup chopped black walnuts
2   teaspoons baking powder
½   teaspoon ground cinnamon
¼   teaspoon salt
⅔   cup skim milk
⅓   cup maple syrup
2½ tablespoons vegetable oil
1   large egg

1. Preheat oven to 400°.

2. Place paper liners coated with cooking spray in muffin cups. Combine flour and next 5 ingredients; make a well in center. Combine remaining ingredients; add to flour mixture. Divide among cups; bake at 400° for 18 minutes. Yield: 12 servings.

POINTS: 3; **Exchanges:** 1½ Starch, 1 Fat
Per serving: CAL 160 (28% from fat); PRO 3.4g; FAT 5g (sat 0.8g); CARB 25.9g; FIB 0.6g; CHOL 18mg; IRON 1.2mg; SOD 65mg; CALC 64mg

Curry-Almond Chicken

3   tablespoons low-salt soy sauce, divided
1½ teaspoons cornstarch, divided
¼   teaspoon salt
1   pound skinned, boned chicken breast, cut
    into bite-size pieces
¼   cup dry sherry
1   tablespoon curry powder
2   tablespoons rice vinegar
1   teaspoon sugar
1   teaspoon dark sesame oil
1   tablespoon vegetable oil
1   cup coarsely chopped yellow bell pepper
½   cup coarsely chopped onion
1   teaspoon peeled minced fresh ginger
3   garlic cloves, minced
1   (8-ounce) can sliced bamboo shoots, drained
4   cups hot cooked long-grain rice
¼   cup sliced green onions
¼   cup slivered almonds, toasted

1. Combine 1 tablespoon soy sauce, ½ teaspoon cornstarch, salt, and chicken. Cover; chill 30 minutes. Combine remaining soy sauce and cornstarch, sherry, and next 4 ingredients.

2. Heat vegetable oil in a nonstick skillet. Add bell pepper and next 3 ingredients; stir-fry 3 minutes; Add chicken mixture; stir-fry 5 minutes. Add sherry mixture and bamboo shoots; stir-fry 1 minute. Serve over rice; top with green onions and almonds. Yield: 4 servings (serving size: 1 cup chicken mixture, 1 cup rice, 1 tablespoon onions, and 1 tablespoon almonds).

POINTS: 10; Exchanges: 4 Starch, 3 Very Lean Meat, 2 Fat
Per serving: CAL 500 (20% from fat); PRO 34g; FAT 10.9g (sat 1.6g); CARB 61.3g; FIB 3.8g; CHOL 66mg; IRON 4.4mg; SOD 591mg; CALC 85mg

Corn-and-Wild Rice Salad

1½ cups uncooked wild rice blend (such as
    Lundberg Farms)
2   cups fresh corn kernels (about 4 ears)
1   cup finely chopped celery
¾   cup shredded carrot
¾   cup dried cranberries (about 3 ounces)
⅔   cup sunflower seeds or unsalted
    pumpkinseed kernels, toasted
½   cup finely chopped red onion
¼   cup raspberry vinegar
1   tablespoon olive oil
1   tablespoon low-salt soy sauce

Curry-Almond Chicken

1   teaspoon grated orange rind
½   teaspoon pepper

1. Cook rice according to package directions, omitting salt and fat. Let cool to room temperature. Combine rice, corn, and remaining ingredients. Cover; chill. Yield: 8 servings (serving size: 1 cup).

POINTS: 5; Exchanges: 3 Starch, 1 Fat
Per serving: CAL 270 (26% from fat); PRO 9.3g; FAT 7.9g (sat 1.4g); CARB 45.3g; FIB 4.6g; CHOL 0mg; IRON 3mg; SOD 78mg; CALC 31mg

Low-Fat Tabbouleh

¾   cup uncooked bulgur or cracked wheat
¾   cup boiling water
1½ cups chopped fresh parsley
¾   cup chopped fresh tomato
½   cup finely chopped red onion
3   tablespoons chopped fresh mint
¼   cup fresh lime juice
2   tablespoons water
1   tablespoon olive oil
½   teaspoon salt
2   garlic cloves, minced

1. Combine bulgur and boiling water; stir well. Let stand at room temperature 30 minutes or until water is absorbed. Add parsley and next 3 ingredients; toss gently. Combine lime juice and next 4 ingredients; stir well. Pour over tabbouleh; cover and chill 3 hours. Toss gently before serving. Yield: 4 servings (serving size: 1 cup).

POINTS: 2; Exchanges: 1½ Starch, ½ Fat
Per serving: CAL 149 (25% from fat); PRO 4.6g; FAT 4.1g (sat 0.6g); CARB 26.6g; FIB 6.6g; CHOL 0mg; IRON 2.3mg; SOD 314mg; CALC 51mg

Flat-leaf or Italian parsley resembles cilantro and has a strong flavor; curly-leaf parsley is more decorative and milder in taste. Parsley is high in vitamin C and carotenes. Add it to salads, pasta, and side dishes, or use it instead of lettuce.

Shopping

Parsley should be bright green in color and show no signs of wilting.

Storage

Wrap washed parsley in paper towels and store it in an unsealed plastic bag in the refrigerator for up to one week. Fresh parsley can also be stored by placing the stems in 1 inch of cold water in a glass. Cover the top with a plastic bag, secure with a rubber band, and change the water every two days.

SUNFLOWER SEEDS

Yes, it's true. By weight sunflower seeds are 47% fat, but they're also 24% protein. And they're one of the best sources of vitamin E and omega-6 linoleic fatty acids, which reduce blood cholesterol. Sunflower seed kernels make a great snack, but they can also be used in breads, cookies, salads, and grain and pasta dishes.

Shopping

Sunflower seeds are available shelled, unshelled, roasted, raw, salted, and unsalted.

Storage

Store raw and unshelled seeds in the refrigerator for up to six months and in the freezer for up to one year; refrigerate roasted seeds for up to four months, or freeze them for up to eight months.

Honey-Sunflower Seed Pancakes

1 cup all-purpose flour
3 tablespoons sunflower seeds
2 teaspoons baking powder
¼ teaspoon salt
¾ cup skim milk
6 tablespoons honey, divided
1 tablespoon vegetable oil
1 large egg
2 fresh peaches, peeled and cut into 12 slices

1. Combine first 4 ingredients in a medium bowl; stir well. Combine milk, 2 tablespoons honey, oil, and egg; stir well. Add to flour mixture, stirring until smooth. Let stand 5 minutes.
2. Spoon about ¼ cup batter for each pancake onto a hot nonstick griddle or skillet. Turn when tops are covered with bubbles and edges look cooked. Serve with remaining honey and peach slices. Yield: 8 servings (serving size: 1 pancake, 1½ teaspoons honey, and 3 peach slices).

POINTS: 3; **Exchanges:** 1½ Starch, ½ Fruit, ½ Fat
Per serving: CAL 166 (23% from fat); PRO 4.1g; FAT 4.2g (sat 0.7g); CARB 29.4g; FIB 1.1g; CHOL 27mg; IRON 1.2mg; SOD 193mg; CALC 84mg

Honey-Apple Glazed Hens With Rice Pilaf

2 (1½-pound) Cornish hens
1 teaspoon olive oil
2 tablespoons chopped onion
2½ cups fat-free chicken broth
1 cup peeled diced Golden Delicious apple (about ½ pound)

Honey-Apple Glazed Hens With Rice Pilaf

⅔ cup uncooked long-grain brown rice
¼ cup uncooked wild rice
2 tablespoons chopped dried apple
½ teaspoon salt
¼ cup honey
2 tablespoons apple juice
1 teaspoon grated lemon rind
1 tablespoon fresh lemon juice
1 teaspoon low-salt soy sauce
Rosemary sprigs (optional)

1. Remove and discard giblets and necks from hens. Rinse hens under cold water; pat dry. Remove skin; trim excess fat. Split hens in half lengthwise; set aside.
2. Heat oil in a saucepan over medium heat. Add onion; sauté 3 minutes. Stir in broth and next 5 ingredients; bring to a boil. Cover, reduce heat, and simmer 1 hour and 10 minutes or until rice is tender and liquid is absorbed. Remove from heat.
3. Preheat oven to 400°.
4. Spoon 4 (¾-cup) mounds of rice mixture onto a jelly-roll pan lined with foil. Place hen halves, meaty sides up, over rice mounds. Combine honey and next 4 ingredients in a bowl; stir well. Brush hens with honey mixture. Bake at 400° for 40 minutes or until juices run clear, basting with honey mixture every 10 minutes. Garnish with rosemary, if desired. Yield: 4 servings.

POINTS: 10; **Exchanges:** 4 Starch, 4 Very Lean Meat
Per serving: CAL 468 (16% from fat); PRO 40.3g; FAT 8.5g (sat 2.2g); CARB 56.6g; FIB 2.5g; CHOL 114mg; IRON 2.3mg; SOD 549mg; CALC 36mg

Italian-Style Shrimp With Lemon and Garlic

2 teaspoons dried Italian seasoning
2 teaspoons Hungarian sweet paprika
2 teaspoons grated lemon rind
½ teaspoon salt
½ teaspoon freshly ground pepper
3 garlic cloves, minced
1 pound large shrimp, peeled and deveined
Cooking spray
4 cups hot cooked angel hair (about 8 ounces uncooked pasta)
2 tablespoons fresh lemon juice
1 tablespoon chopped fresh parsley
Lemon zest (optional)

1. Combine Italian seasoning and next 5 ingredients in a medium bowl; stir well. Add shrimp; toss well to coat. Thread shrimp evenly onto each of 4 (8-inch) skewers.

2. Place kebabs on a broiler pan coated with cooking spray, and broil 2 minutes on each side. Remove shrimp from skewers; arrange over angel hair pasta. Drizzle with lemon juice; sprinkle with parsley. Garnish with lemon zest, if desired. Yield: 4 servings (serving size: 3 ounces shrimp and 1 cup pasta).

POINTS: 6; **Exchanges**: 2 Very Lean Meat, 3 Starch
Per serving: CAL 302 (8% from fat); PRO 24.5g; FAT 2.8g (sat 0.5g); CARB 43.6g; FIB 2.8g; CHOL 129mg; IRON 5.3mg; SOD 422mg; CALC 86mg

Monterey Jack-and-Poblano Chicken Roll-up

2 fresh poblano chiles (about ½ pound)
4 (4-ounce) skinned, boned chicken breast halves
1 teaspoon dried Italian seasoning
1 teaspoon pepper
¼ teaspoon salt
¼ teaspoon garlic powder
1 (2-ounce) piece reduced-fat Monterey Jack cheese, cut into 4 strips
¼ cup all-purpose flour
¼ cup Italian-seasoned breadcrumbs
1 large egg, lightly beaten
2 teaspoons stick margarine
Cooking spray

Dinner is ready in 30 minutes with Italian-Style Shrimp With Lemon and Garlic

1. Cut poblano chiles in half lengthwise; discard seeds and membranes. Place pepper halves, skin side up, on a foil-lined baking sheet; flatten with hand. Broil 15 minutes or until blackened. Place in a zip-top plastic bag; seal bag, and let stand 5 minutes. Peel chiles, and set aside.

2. Place each chicken breast half between 2 sheets of heavy-duty plastic wrap; flatten to ¼-inch thickness using a meat mallet or rolling pin. Sprinkle Italian seasoning and next 3 ingredients evenly over chicken; place 1 chile half lengthwise over each chicken breast. Place 1 strip of cheese crosswise at one end of each chicken breast; roll up chicken and chile jelly-roll fashion to enclose cheese. Tuck in sides of chicken, and secure each roll with wooden picks.

3. Combine flour and breadcrumbs in a shallow dish. Dip each chicken roll in egg; dredge in flour mixture. Place chicken rolls in an 8-inch square baking dish; cover and chill 1 hour.

4. Preheat oven to 400°.

5. Melt margarine in a large nonstick skillet over medium heat. Add chicken rolls, and cook until browned on all sides, turning occasionally. Return chicken to 8-inch square baking dish coated with cooking spray; bake at 400° for 25 minutes or until done. Yield: 4 servings.

Note: You may substitute 1 (4-ounce) can whole green chiles, halved and seeded, for the fresh poblano chiles, if desired. Use 1 green chile half per chicken breast half.

POINTS: 7; **Exchanges:** 1 Starch, 4 Very Lean Meat, 1 Fat, ½ Med-fat Meat
Per serving: CAL 305 (30% from fat); PRO 35g; FAT 10.3g (sat 3.5g); CARB 17.3g; FIB 1.5g; CHOL 135mg; IRON 2.9mg; SOD 544mg; CALC 165mg

Blueberry-Ginger Cheesecake

Cooking spray
¼ cup gingersnap crumbs (about 8 cookies, finely crushed)
¾ cup sugar
2 (8-ounce) tubs light cream cheese
2 cups fat-free sour cream
2 tablespoons ginger-flavored liqueur (optional)
2 tablespoons minced crystallized ginger
5 large egg whites
1 large egg yolk
¼ cup sugar
¼ cup water
1 tablespoon cornstarch
3 cups fresh blueberries
2 teaspoons minced crystallized ginger

1. Preheat oven to 325°.

2. Coat bottom of a 10-inch springform pan with cooking spray; sprinkle with gingersnap cookie crumbs. Set aside.

STEP BY STEP: GRATING AND CHOPPING GINGER

To grate fresh ginger, peel and then cut a piece big enough to hold comfortably while using a fine grater.

▼

Chop according to recipe instructions

▼

▲

Peel the outer skin with a paring knife. Be careful: The flesh just below is the most flavorful.

To chop fresh ginger, first crush it under the flat side of a knife.

▲

3. Combine ¾ cup sugar and cream cheese in a food processor; process until smooth. Add sour cream and liqueur, if desired; process until blended. Add 2 tablespoons crystallized ginger, egg whites, and egg yolk; pulse until blended. Pour batter into prepared pan. Bake at 325° for 45 minutes or until almost set. Remove from oven; let cool 2 hours on a wire rack.

4. Combine ¼ cup sugar, water, and cornstarch in a medium saucepan; stir until well blended. Stir in fresh blueberries and 2 teaspoons crystallized ginger; bring to a boil. Cook 1 minute, stirring constantly. Remove from heat, and let cool completely. Spread blueberry mixture evenly over cheesecake. Cover and chill at least 8 hours. Yield: 12 servings (serving size: 1 wedge).

Note: You can find crystallized ginger in the spice section of most large grocery stores. Canton-brand ginger-flavored liqueur is available in liquor stores but may be omitted.

POINTS: 5; **Exchanges:** 2 Starch, 1½ Fat
Per serving: CAL 237 (30% from fat); PRO 8.9g; FAT 7.9g (sat 4.2g); CARB 32.3g; FIB 1.7g; CHOL 42mg; IRON 0.7mg; SOD 274mg; CALC 68mg

Almond-Rice Pilaf

4	cups hot cooked rice
¼	cup sliced green onions
2	tablespoons sliced almonds, toasted
1	teaspoon low-salt soy sauce
¼	teaspoon salt

1. Combine all ingredients; toss well. Yield: 4 servings (serving size: 1 cup).

POINTS: 4; **Exchanges:** 3 Starch
Per serving: CAL 222 (9% from fat); PRO 4.8g; FAT 2.3g (sat 0.3g); CARB 44.1g; FIB 1.4g; CHOL 0mg; IRON 2.2mg; SOD 185mg; CALC 47mg

Gingered Flounder

⅔	cup peeled grated fresh ginger
2	tablespoons low-salt soy sauce
2	tablespoons dry sherry
2	tablespoons lemon juice
2	teaspoons sugar
4	(6-ounce) flounder fillets
Cooking spray	
1	teaspoon dark sesame oil

1. Place ginger on several layers of damp cheesecloth, and gather edges of cheesecloth together. Squeeze cheesecloth bag over a small bowl. Set aside 3 tablespoons ginger juice.

2. Combine 2 tablespoons ginger juice, soy sauce, sherry, lemon juice, and sugar in a large zip-top plastic bag. Add fish; seal bag, and marinate in refrigerator 20 minutes, turning bag occasionally. Remove fish from bag, and discard marinade.

3. Place fish on a broiler pan coated with cooking spray; broil 3 minutes or until lightly browned (do not turn). Brush sesame oil over fish, and broil an additional minute or until fish flakes easily when tested with a fork. Place fish on individual serving plates, and drizzle remaining tablespoon ginger juice over fish. Yield: 4 servings (serving size: 1 fillet).

POINTS: 4; **Exchanges:** 4½ Very Lean Meat, ½ Fat
Per serving: CAL 191 (19% from fat); PRO 31g; FAT 4g (sat 0.7g); CARB 5g; FIB 0g; CHOL 87mg; IRON 0.5mg; SOD 427mg; CALC 25mg

Earl Grey Sorbet

This grown-up, not-too-sweet sorbet is wonderful served as a palate cleanser between courses or as a dessert after a rich meal.

2	cups boiling water
⅔	cup sugar
¼	cup loose Earl Grey tea
½	cup fresh lemon juice

1. Combine boiling water, sugar, and loose Earl Grey tea in a medium bowl, and stir well. Cover tea mixture and steep 5 minutes. Strain tea mixture through a fine sieve into a bowl, and discard tea leaves. Stir lemon juice into tea. Cover and chill.

2. Pour tea into freezer can of an ice-cream freezer, and freeze according to manufacturer's instructions. Spoon sorbet into a freezer-safe container; cover and freeze sorbet 3 hours. Yield: 10 servings (serving size: ½ cup).

POINTS: 1; **Exchanges:** 1 Fruit
Per serving: CAL 57 (0% from fat); PRO 0.1g; FAT 0g (sat 0g); CARB 14.9g; FIB 0g; CHOL 0mg; IRON 0mg; SOD 1mg; CALC 1mg

Fresh ginger has been credited with everything from fighting colds to combating nausea. It is also a powerful tool for the health-conscious cook: Its scent and bite lend curries, stir-fries, and many ethnic dishes a spicy warmth.

Shopping

Fresh ginger is available year-round at most grocery stores. Make sure that its smooth, tan-colored skin has no cracks or wrinkles.

Storage

Store unpeeled ginger in an airtight container in the refrigerator for up to three weeks. Or freeze it for up to a year covered in plastic wrap and inside a freezer-safe bag. Store crystallized ginger at room temperature in an airtight container for up to one year.

Super Sea Foods

Although people have been eating seafood since oceans
and humans have coexisted, new health benefits
of a fish-rich diet are discovered every day.

W*e're not sure how it works, but apparently carbon dating of skeletons has shown that cavemen ate salmon 100 million years ago. Could be their moms told them what our moms told us—that the iodine in fish would make us smarter. Could be salmon were easier to catch than dinosaurs. Could be they were just hungry. It doesn't really matter. The point is, we should follow their lead. It's true that seafood is rich in iodine, which is vital to our ability to think. But more importantly, fish is the richest food source of omega-3 fatty acids. Research has shown that omega-3s may reduce the risk of death from heart attack by preventing blood clots or keeping other fats from damaging artery walls. One study found that men who ate two servings of fatty fish a week had a lower rate of heart attacks than men who either reduced their fat intake to no more than 30% of their total calories or increased their dietary fiber to 16 grams a day. Omega-3s may also strengthen your defenses against stroke and rheumatoid arthritis and may help combat high blood pressure and some types of cancer, including breast cancer. Of course, seafood is also high in protein and relatively low in calories. So, how do you like your salmon?*

**Mussels Marinara
is seafood with an
Italian accent.**

Broiled Scallop Gratin

Mussels Marinara

1 tablespoon olive oil
1 cup finely chopped onion
3 garlic cloves, minced
2 cups chopped tomato
½ cup dry white wine
⅓ cup chopped fresh flat-leaf parsley
2 tablespoons chopped fresh basil
½ teaspoon salt
½ teaspoon black pepper
¼ teaspoon crushed red pepper
2 bay leaves
5 pounds fresh mussels, scrubbed and debearded (about 100 mussels)
5 cups hot cooked linguine (about 10 ounces uncooked pasta)
Basil sprigs (optional)

1. Heat oil in a large stockpot over medium-high heat. Add onion and garlic; sauté 3 minutes. Add tomato and next 7 ingredients; cook over medium heat 5 minutes. Add mussels; cover and cook 10 minutes or until mussels open. Discard bay leaves and any unopened shells.

2. Spoon linguine into each of 5 individual shallow bowls. Remove mussels from pan with a slotted spoon, and arrange over pasta. Spoon tomato mixture over mussels. Garnish with basil sprigs, if desired. Yield: 5 servings (serving size: 1 cup pasta, about 20 mussels, ½ cup sauce).

POINTS: 6; **Exchanges:** 1 Very Lean Meat, 3 Starch, ½ Fat
Per serving: CAL 305 (17% from fat); PRO 16g; FAT 5.6g (sat 0.9g); CARB 47.6g; FIB 4.1g; CHOL 20mg; IRON 5.8mg; SOD 451mg; CALC 56mg

Broiled Scallop Gratin

⅓ cup fresh lime juice
¼ cup minced fresh parsley
¼ cup minced red bell pepper
¼ cup minced green onions
1½ tablespoons Southwestern-style oil with garlic, jalapeño pepper, cilantro, and lime or 1½ tablespoons olive oil
¼ teaspoon salt
1½ pounds sea scallops
Cilantro sprigs (optional)

1. Combine all ingredients except cilantro in a bowl; stir well. Divide scallop mixture evenly among 4 individual gratin dishes. Place dishes on a baking sheet; broil 10 minutes or until scallops are done. Garnish with cilantro sprigs, if desired. Yield: 4 servings.

POINTS: 4; **Exchanges:** 2½ Very Lean Meat, 1 Fat, ½ Starch
Per serving: CAL 156 (35% from fat); PRO 19.4g; FAT 6g (sat 0.8g); CARB 5.7g; FIB 0.5g; CHOL 37mg; IRON 0.8mg; SOD 333mg; CALC 40mg

Dungeness Crab Cakes

2 medium red potatoes, peeled
2 tablespoons light mayonnaise
1½ teaspoons fresh lemon juice
¼ teaspoon dry mustard
¾ teaspoon grated lemon rind
⅛ teaspoon salt
⅛ teaspoon hot pepper sauce
2 large egg whites, lightly beaten
3 tablespoons minced fresh parsley
2 tablespoons finely chopped celery
1 tablespoon finely chopped green onions
½ pound Dungeness or lump crabmeat, shell pieces removed
½ cup dry breadcrumbs
2 teaspoons vegetable oil, divided
Lemon wedges

1. Place potatoes in a saucepan, and cover with water; bring to a boil. Reduce heat, and simmer 15 minutes or until tender; drain. Let cool; cover and chill. Coarsely shred potatoes.

2. Combine mayonnaise and next 6 ingredients in a medium bowl; stir well. Add shredded potato, parsley, and next 3 ingredients; stir well. Divide mixture into 6 equal portions, shaping each into a ½-inch-thick patty. Place breadcrumbs in a pie plate or shallow dish, and dredge patties in breadcrumbs.

3. Heat 1 teaspoon oil in a nonstick skillet over medium heat. Add 3 patties; cook 3 minutes. Turn patties over; cook an additional 3 minutes or until golden. Remove patties from skillet; set aside, and keep warm. Repeat with remaining oil and patties. Serve with lemon wedges. Yield: 6 servings (serving size: 1 crab cake).

POINTS: 3; **Exchanges:** 1 Starch, 1 Very Lean Meat, ½ Fat
Per serving: CAL 144 (24% from fat); PRO 10.9g; FAT 3.8g (sat 0.8g); CARB 15.5g; FIB 1.3g; CHOL 38mg; IRON 1.4mg; SOD 310mg; CALC 69mg

Shopping

Buy mussels with tightly closed shells or those that quickly close when tapped. Shells that feel heavy are probably full of sand, and those that feel light are probably home to a dead mussel. Shucked mussels should be plump and surrounded by clear liquid. Small mussels are more tender than large ones.

Storage

Keep live mussels in a single layer covered with a moist cloth in the refrigerator. Refrigerate shucked mussels completely covered in their liquor or in water in an airtight container for no more than two days.

OYSTERS

Creole Oyster Po'Boy

New Orleans legend has it that this sandwich was brought home by mischievous husbands to placate their wives, so it was nicknamed "The Peacemaker."

⅓ cup cornmeal
⅓ cup dry breadcrumbs
½ teaspoon garlic powder
¼ teaspoon salt
¼ teaspoon ground red pepper
¼ teaspoon black pepper
2 tablespoons low-fat buttermilk
1 large egg white
2 (10-ounce) containers standard oysters, drained
Cooking spray
1 (1-pound) loaf French bread (about 16 inches long)
Creole Mayonnaise
2 cups thinly sliced iceberg lettuce
24 thin tomato slices

1. Combine first 6 ingredients in a pie plate or shallow dish, and stir well. Combine buttermilk and egg white in a bowl, and stir well. Dip oysters in buttermilk mixture; dredge in cornmeal mixture. Coat a large nonstick skillet with cooking spray, and place over medium heat until hot. Add oysters, and cook 3 minutes on each side or until browned.

2. Cut bread loaf in half horizontally, and spread Creole Mayonnaise evenly over cut sides of bread. Arrange lettuce and tomato slices over bottom half of loaf, and top with oysters and top half of loaf. Cut loaf into 8 pieces. Serve immediately. Yield: 8 sandwiches.

POINTS: 6; **Exchanges:** 3 Starch, ½ Very Lean Meat, ½ Fat **Per serving:** CAL 285 (15% from fat); PRO 11.5g; FAT 4.8g (sat 1.3g); CARB 46.3g; FIB 2.6g; CHOL 35mg; IRON 6.1mg; SOD 655mg; CALC 74mg

Creole Mayonnaise:

¼ cup light mayonnaise
1 tablespoon minced green onions
1 tablespoon minced fresh parsley
2 teaspoons sweet pickle relish
2 teaspoons Creole or other coarse-grained mustard
1 teaspoon capers
½ teaspoon hot sauce

1. Combine all ingredients in a bowl; stir well. Yield: ⅓ cup (serving size: 2 teaspoons).

Oyster Artichoke Soufflés

Cooking spray
¼ cup minced shallots
4 cups chopped fresh spinach leaves
1 (14-ounce) can artichoke hearts, drained and coarsely chopped
1 tablespoon cornstarch
1 cup skim milk
2 large egg yolks
¼ cup (1 ounce) grated fresh Parmesan cheese
⅛ teaspoon pepper
2 (8-ounce) cans boiled whole oysters, drained and coarsely chopped
4 large egg whites (at room temperature)

1. Preheat oven to 400°.

2. Coat a nonstick skillet with cooking spray; place over medium heat until hot. Add shallots, and sauté 2 minutes. Add spinach; sauté 30 seconds or until spinach begins to wilt. Stir in artichokes. Coat 6 (6-ounce) custard cups or a 1½-quart soufflé dish with cooking spray; divide mixture among dishes. Set aside.

Creole Oyster Po'Boy

3. Place cornstarch in a saucepan. Gradually add skim milk, stirring with a whisk until blended. Bring mixture to a boil over medium heat, and cook 1 minute or until thick and bubbly, stirring constantly.

4. Place 2 egg yolks in a bowl; beat with a whisk. Gradually stir about one-fourth of hot milk mixture into yolks; add to remaining hot mixture, stirring constantly. Add cheese, pepper, and oysters; cook an additional 2 minutes, stirring frequently. Pour into a bowl; set aside.

5. Beat 4 egg whites at high speed of a mixer until stiff peaks form. Stir one-fourth of egg whites into oyster mixture; fold remaining egg whites into oyster mixture. Spoon evenly over spinach mixture in dishes; place dishes on a baking sheet. Bake at 400° for 10 minutes. Reduce oven temperature to 350°, and bake soufflés 15 minutes or until puffed and set. Serve immediately. Yield: 6 servings.

POINTS: 3; **Exchanges:** 2 Veg, 1½ Lean Meat
Per serving: CAL 151 (30% from fat); PRO 13.5g; FAT 5.1g (sat 1.7g, mono 1.1g, poly 0.9g); CARB 13.2g; FIB 1.9g; CHOL 116mg; IRON 7mg; SOD 362mg; CALC 195mg

Lemon-Peppered Salmon and Vegetables

2   tablespoons fresh lemon juice
1   tablespoon Dijon mustard
2   teaspoons vegetable oil
½   teaspoon coarsely ground pepper
2   garlic cloves, minced
1½ cups sliced yellow squash
2   (6-ounce) salmon fillets (½ inch thick)
1   medium leek (about ½ pound), trimmed
    and halved
4   broccoli spears
Lemon wedges (optional)

1. Combine first 5 ingredients in a small bowl; stir well. Combine 1 tablespoon mustard mixture and squash in a medium bowl; toss well, and set aside. Spread remaining mustard mixture evenly over salmon fillets.

2. Add water to a Dutch oven to a depth of 1-inch. Line a vegetable steamer with foil, and place in Dutch oven. Arrange leek halves in steamer, and steam, covered, 4 minutes. Add broccoli to steamer, and steam, covered, 2 minutes. Arrange squash over broccoli; top with salmon. Steam, covered, an additional 5 minutes or until fish flakes easily when tested with a fork (add additional boiling water to pan if needed). Divide salmon and vegetables evenly between 2 plates; drizzle evenly with juices from foil. Serve with lemon wedges, if desired. Yield: 2 servings (serving size: 1 salmon fillet, 2 broccoli spears, 1 leek half, and ½ cup squash).

POINTS: 6; **Exchanges:** 3 Veg, 1 Fat, 3 Lean Meat
Per serving: CAL 298 (37% from fat); PRO 28.7g; FAT 12.4g (SAT 2.5g); CARB 19g; FIB 3.2g; CHOL 44mg; IRON 3.1mg; SOD 300mg; CALC 98mg

Grilled Salmon Pepper Steaks

2   tablespoons cracked pepper
6   (6-ounce) salmon steaks
⅔   cup rice vinegar
2   tablespoons fresh lemon juice
2   tablespoons Dijon mustard
1   tablespoon dark sesame oil

Steaming is perfect for simple recipes, such as Lemon-Peppered Salmon and Vegetables.

¼ teaspoon salt
⅛ teaspoon pepper
4 garlic cloves, minced
Cooking spray
¼ teaspoon cornstarch

1. Press cracked pepper into both sides of salmon steaks; place steaks in a large shallow dish. Combine vinegar and next 6 ingredients; stir well, and pour over steaks. Cover and marinate in refrigerator 1 hour, turning steaks occasionally.

2. Prepare grill. Remove steaks from dish, reserving marinade. Place steaks on grill rack coated with cooking spray; grill 5 minutes on each side or until fish flakes easily when tested with a fork, basting frequently with half of reserved marinade. Combine cornstarch and remaining half of marinade in a small saucepan; stir until well blended. Bring to a boil; cook 1 minute or until thick, stirring constantly with a whisk. Spoon about 1 tablespoon sauce over each steak. Yield: 6 servings.

POINTS: 7; **Exchanges:** 4½ Lean Meat, ½ Fat
Per serving: CAL 280 (48% from fat); PRO 30.6g; FAT 14.9g (sat 2.5g); CARB 3.8g; FIB 0.6g; CHOL 96mg; IRON 1.3mg; SOD 321mg; CALC 21mg

Sardine Pâté Appetizers

2 (3¾-ounce) cans sardines in water, drained
¼ cup minced green onions
¼ cup plain fat-free yogurt
1 tablespoon lemon juice
1 teaspoon dried dill
1½ teaspoons prepared horseradish
30 pieces melba toast
⅓ cup finely shredded carrot

1. Place sardines in a bowl; mash with a fork. Add onions and next 4 ingredients; stir well. Cover and chill at least 2 hours. Spread 2 teaspoons over each melba toast; top with about ½ teaspoon carrot. Yield: 2½ dozen (serving size: 1 appetizer).

POINTS: 1; **Exchanges:** ½ Starch
Per serving: CAL 30 (30% from fat); PRO 1.8g; FAT 1g (sat 0.3g); CARB 3.4g; FIB 0.1g; CHOL 4mg; IRON 0.3mg; SOD 67mg; CALC 20mg

Herring Sandwiches

1   teaspoon coarse-grained mustard
2   (2½-ounce) hoagie or submarine rolls,
    split
1   (8-ounce) jar herring in wine sauce,
    drained
8   (¼-inch-thick) slices cucumber
2   (½-inch-thick) slices tomato
2   (¼-inch-thick) slices onion

1. Spread mustard evenly over bottom halves of rolls, and top with herring, cucumber, tomato, onion, and roll tops. Serve immediately. Yield: 2 servings.

POINTS: 9; **Exchanges:** 3½ Starch, 1½ Lean Meat, 1 Fat
Per serving: CAL 417 (26% from fat); PRO 21.3g; FAT 12g (sat 1.8g); CARB 56.4g; FIB 0.9g; CHOL 45mg; IRON 3.3mg; SOD 1,221mg; CALC 27mg

New England Clam Chowder

2   (44-ounce) cans steamer clams in shells,
    undrained
Cooking spray
3   cups chopped onion
2   cups cubed red potato (about 1½ pounds)
1   cup diced celery
2   turkey-bacon slices, chopped
2   cups water
½   teaspoon salt
½   teaspoon dried thyme
¼   teaspoon coarsely ground pepper
3   fresh parsley sprigs
1   bay leaf
3   tablespoons all-purpose flour
2   cups 2% reduced-fat milk

1. Drain clams, reserving 1 cup clam liquid. Remove clams from shells; discard shells. Slip black skin off foot of each clam, and discard. Set clams aside.
2. Coat a Dutch oven with cooking spray; place over medium-high heat until hot. Add onion, potato, celery, and bacon; sauté 7 minutes. Add reserved clam liquid, water, and next 5 ingredients; bring to a boil. Cover, reduce heat, and simmer 20 minutes or until potato is tender. Discard parsley and bay leaf.
3. Place flour in a bowl. Gradually add milk, blending with a whisk; add to pan. Cook over

medium heat 10 minutes or until thick, stirring frequently. Stir in clams; cook 2 minutes or until heated. Yield: 9 servings (serving size: 1 cup).
Note: Substitute 2 pounds fresh clams in shells and 1 (8-ounce) bottle of clam juice for the 2 cans of steamer clams and 1 cup drained clam liquid, if desired.

POINTS: 2; **Exchanges:** 1 Starch, 1 Very Lean Meat, ½ Fat
Per serving: CAL 130 (21% from fat); PRO 8.4g; FAT 3.1g (sat 1.1g, mono 1.1g, poly 0.6g); CARB 16.6g; FIB 1.9g; CHOL 21mg; IRON 4.2mg; SOD 398mg; CALC 103mg

Mussel, Clam, and Cheddar Pizza

2   cups water
25 small fresh mussels, scrubbed and
    debearded
1   teaspoon olive oil
½   cup chopped shallot
3   garlic cloves, minced
¼   cup dry white wine
⅛   teaspoon ground red pepper
⅛   teaspoon black pepper
1   (6½-ounce) can minced clams,
    undrained
2   tablespoons chopped fresh parsley
15 large fresh spinach leaves
1   (12-inch) Cornmeal Pizza Crust
½   cup (2 ounces) shredded white cheddar
    cheese
¼   cup shredded fresh Parmesan cheese

1. Preheat oven to 500°.
2. Bring 2 cups water to a boil in a large Dutch oven; add mussels. Cover and steam 2 minutes or until shells open; discard any unopened shells. Remove meat from shells; set aside. Discard shells.
3. Heat oil in a medium nonstick skillet over medium heat. Add shallots and garlic; sauté 2 minutes or until tender. Add wine and next 3 ingredients; cook 9 minutes or until most of liquid evaporates, stirring occasionally. Remove from heat; stir in mussels and parsley.
4. Arrange spinach leaves over prepared crust, leaving a ½-inch border. Sprinkle cheddar cheese over spinach; top with clam mixture. Sprinkle with Parmesan cheese. Bake at 500° for 10 min-

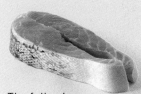

Shopping

Look for live, hard-shell clams with tightly closed shells. If the shell is slightly open, tap lightly. It should quickly snap shut; if it doesn't, discard it. When shopping for soft-shell clams, lightly touch the neck; it should move. If it doesn't, don't buy it. Shucked clams should be plump and surrounded by clear liquid.

Storage

Keep live clams in an open container covered with a damp cloth for up to two days in a 40° refrigerator. Shucked clams can be stored in their liquor or in water in an airtight container and refrigerated up to three days or frozen up to three months.

utes on bottom rack of oven. Remove pizza to a cutting board; let stand 5 minutes. Yield: 6 servings (serving size: 1 wedge).

POINTS: 6; **Exchanges:** 2 Starch, 1 Fat, 1½ Lean Meat, 1 Veg
Per serving: CAL 288 (21% from fat) PRO 13.8g; FAT 6.7g (sat 3g, mono 2.3g, poly 0.6g); CARB 42.3g; FIB 2.4g; CHOL 27mg; IRON 4.8mg; SOD 455mg; CALC 160mg

Cornmeal Pizza Crust:

1   tablespoon sugar
1   package dry yeast
¾   cup warm water (105° to 115°)
1⅔ cups all-purpose flour, divided
½   cup yellow cornmeal
½   teaspoon olive oil
¼   teaspoon salt
Cooking spray
1½ teaspoons yellow cornmeal

1. Dissolve sugar and yeast in ¾ cup warm water in a large bowl; let stand 5 minutes. Add 1⅓ cups flour, cornmeal, olive oil, and salt to form a soft dough.

2. Turn dough out onto a lightly floured surface. Knead until smooth and elastic (about 5 minutes); add enough of remaining flour, one tablespoon at a time, to prevent dough from sticking to hands.

3. Place dough in a large bowl coated with cooking spray, turning to coat top. Cover and let rise in a warm place (85°), free from drafts, 45 minutes or until doubled in bulk. Punch dough down, and roll into a 12-inch circle on a floured surface. Coat a 12-inch pizza pan or baking sheet with cooking spray, and sprinkle with 1½ teaspoons cornmeal. Place dough on prepared baking sheet. Crimp dough edges with fingers to form a rim. Cover and let rise in a warm place (85°), free from drafts, 30 minutes. Yield: 1 (12-inch) pizza crust.

Minestrone With Clams

1   cup dried baby lima beans
1   tablespoon olive oil
2   cups finely chopped onion
1   teaspoon fennel seeds, crushed
1   teaspoon dried thyme

3   garlic cloves, minced
5   (10½-ounce) cans low-salt chicken broth
2   cups diced zucchini
1   cup uncooked small seashell macaroni
½   cup chopped fresh flat-leaf parsley
¾   teaspoon grated lemon rind
¼   teaspoon salt
¼   teaspoon crushed red pepper
1   (10-ounce) can whole baby clams
5   tablespoons grated Parmesan cheese
Fresh clams (optional)

1. Sort and wash lima beans, and place in a large Dutch oven. Cover with water to 2 inches above beans, and bring to a boil; cook 2 minutes. Remove from heat; cover and let stand 1 hour. Drain beans.

2. Heat olive oil in pan over medium heat. Add onion, fennel seeds, thyme, and minced garlic; sauté 5 minutes. Add beans and chicken broth, and bring mixture to a boil. Cover, reduce heat, and simmer 1 hour. Add diced zucchini and next 6 ingredients; cook 15 minutes or until pasta is done. Ladle soup into individual soup bowls, and sprinkle each with ½ tablespoon Parmesan cheese. Garnish with fresh clams, if desired. Yield: 10 servings (serving size: 1 cup soup and ½ tablespoon cheese).

POINTS: 3; **Exchanges:** 1 Starch, ½ Fat, 1 Very Lean Meat
Per serving: CAL 138 (24% from fat); PRO 8.2g; FAT 3.7g (sat 0.8g, mono 1.3g, poly 0.3g): CARB 18.4g; FIB 2g; CHOL 11mg; IRON 3.4mg; SOD 323mg; CALC 79mg

Sardine Sandwiches With Horseradish-Dill Dressing

1   (3¾-ounce) can sardines in water, drained
⅓   cup plain fat-free yogurt
2   tablespoons light mayonnaise
1   tablespoon prepared horseradish
½   teaspoon dried dill
4   (1-ounce) slices pumpernickel bread
2   Boston lettuce leaves
4   (¼-inch-thick) slices tomato
6   (⅛-inch-thick) rings red onion

1. Split each sardine in half lengthwise. Discard bones, if desired; set aside.

2. Combine yogurt, mayonnaise, horseradish, and dill in a bowl; stir well. Spread 1 tablespoon yogurt mixture over bread slices. Divide lettuce, tomato, onion, and sardines evenly between 2 bread slices. Drizzle 2 tablespoons yogurt mixture over each sandwich; top with remaining bread. Yield: 2 servings.

POINTS: 6; **Exchanges:** 2 Starch, 1 Fat, 1½ Lean Meat, 1 Veg
Per serving: CAL 309 (33% from fat); PRO 16.8g; FAT 11.3g (sat 2.2g); CARB 36.9g; FIB 4.7g; CHOL 39mg; IRON 3.1mg; SOD 694mg; CALC 267mg

Lobster Tails With Chunky Tomato Vinaigrette

4   (6- or 7-ounce) lobster tails
1   tablespoon balsamic vinegar
1   tablespoon water
½   teaspoon olive oil
¼   teaspoon dried tarragon
Chunky Tomato Vinaigrette

1. Cut lengthwise through top of lobster shell (with kitchen shears), and press shell open. Starting at large end of tail, carefully loosen lobster meat from bottom of shell, keeping meat attached at end of tail. Lift meat through the top shell opening, and place on top of shell. Repeat procedure with remaining lobster tails. Place lobster tails on a broiler pan.
2. Combine vinegar, water, oil, and tarragon; stir well. Brush lobster with half of vinegar mixture.
3. Broil 10 minutes or until lobster flesh turns opaque, basting with remaining vinegar mixture after 5 minutes. Serve with Chunky Tomato Vinaigrette. Yield: 4 servings (serving size: 6 tablespoons vinaigrette).

POINTS: 2; **Exchanges:** 3 Very Lean Meat, ½ Fat
Per serving: CAL 121 (21% from fat); PRO 19.4g; FAT 2.8g (sat 0.5g); CARB 4.3g; FIB 1.1g; CHOL 94mg; IRON 1mg; SOD 405mg; CALC 64mg

Minestrone With Clams is a trattoria classic.

¼ cup all-purpose flour
2 cups 2% reduced-fat milk
2½ tablespoons tomato paste
¼ teaspoon salt
Dash of ground red pepper
1 tablespoon dry sherry
2 tablespoons chopped celery leaves
(optional)

1. Remove meat from cooked lobster tail and claws. Chop meat, and set aside. Place lobster shell in a large heavy-duty zip-top plastic bag. Coarsely crush the shell using a meat mallet or rolling pin. Place crushed shell in a large sauce-pan; add water and next 3 ingredients. Partially cover, and cook over medium-low heat 30 minutes. Strain shell mixture through a sieve over a bowl, reserving stock. Discard shell pieces, cloves, and bay leaf.

2. Melt margarine in pan coated with cooking spray over medium heat. Add chopped onion and celery, and sauté 3 minutes. Sprinkle flour over onion mixture; stir well, and cook 1 minute, stirring constantly.

3. Add the reserved lobster stock, milk, tomato paste, salt, and red pepper gradually; cook over medium heat 8 minutes or until thick, stirring constantly. Stir in chopped lobster meat, and cook 1 minute, stirring constantly. Remove from heat, and stir in sherry. Garnish with chopped celery leaves, if desired. Yield: 4 servings (serving size: 1 cup).

POINTS: 3; **Exchanges:** ½ Starch, 1 Very Lean Meat, ½ Fat, ½ Low-Fat Milk
Per serving: CAL 152 (29% from fat); PRO11g; FAT 4.9g (sat 1.9g); CARB 15.5g; FIB 1g; CHOL 37mg; IRON 0.9mg; SOD 367mg; CALC 171mg

The stock made from lobster shells gives Lobster Bisque its rich flavor.

Chunky Tomato Vinaigrette:

1½ cups peeled finely chopped tomato
(about 2 medium)
2 tablespoons minced green onions
2 tablespoons finely chopped fresh
parsley
1 tablespoon balsamic vinegar
1 teaspoon water
1 teaspoon olive oil
½ teaspoon dried tarragon
⅛ teaspoon salt
⅛ teaspoon pepper

1. Combine all ingredients in a bowl; stir well. Cover and chill 1 hour. Yield: 1½ cups (serving size: 6 tablespoons).

Lobster Bisque

1 (1¼-pound) whole Maine lobster,
cooked
1¼ cups water
1 (8-ounce) bottle clam juice
2 whole cloves
1 bay leaf
2 teaspoons margarine
Cooking spray
¼ cup finely chopped onion
¼ cup finely chopped celery

Roasted Corn-and-Lobster Chowder

2 tablespoons olive oil, divided
4 ears corn
2 (1½-pound) whole Maine lobsters,
cooked
1 cup finely chopped onion
1 cup finely chopped leek

¾ cup finely chopped celery
3 garlic cloves, minced
¼ cup all-purpose flour
3 (10½-ounce) cans low-salt chicken broth
3 cups cubed Yukon gold or red potatoes (about 1 pound)
2 fresh thyme sprigs
1 fresh parsley sprig
1 bay leaf
2 cups evaporated skim milk
1 tablespoon brown sugar
¾ teaspoon salt
¼ teaspoon ground nutmeg
¼ teaspoon pepper

1. Brush 1 teaspoon olive oil over ears of corn. Prepare grill or broiler, and place corn on grill rack or broiler pan. Cook 20 minutes or until the corn is lightly browned, turning every 5 minutes, and let cool. Cut kernels from cobs to measure 3 cups, reserving 2 cobs, and set corn kernels aside.

2. Remove meat from cooked lobster tails and claws, and coarsely chop meat to measure 1½ cups; set aside.

3. Heat remaining 5 teaspoons olive oil in a large Dutch oven over medium heat. Add onion, leek, celery, and garlic; sauté 5 minutes or until tender. Sprinkle flour over onion mixture; stir well, and cook for 1 minute, stirring constantly.

4. Add chicken broth gradually, stirring with a whisk until well blended. Add reserved corn cobs, potato, thyme, parsley, and bay leaf; cover, reduce heat, and simmer 5 minutes. Stir in corn kernels and milk; cover and simmer 10 minutes or until potato is tender. Discard corn cobs, thyme, parsley, and bay leaf. Add lobster meat, brown sugar, and remaining ingredients; simmer, uncovered, 2 minutes. Yield: 11 servings (serving size: 1 cup).

POINTS: 3; **Exchanges:** 1½ Starch, ½ Skim Milk, ½ Very Lean Meat
Per serving: CAL 179 (19% from fat); PRO 12.2g; FAT 3.7g (sat 0.6g, mono 2.2g, poly 0.5g); CARB 25.4g; FIB 2.1g; CHOL 21mg; IRON 1.6mg; SOD 360mg; CALC 173mg

Greek-Style Scampi

1 teaspoon olive oil
5 garlic cloves, minced
3 (28-ounce) cans whole tomatoes, drained and coarsely chopped
½ cup chopped fresh parsley, divided
1¼ pounds large shrimp, peeled and deveined
1 cup (4 ounces) crumbled feta cheese
2 tablespoons fresh lemon juice
¼ teaspoon freshly ground pepper

1. Preheat oven to 400°.

2. Heat oil in a large Dutch oven over medium heat. Add garlic; sauté 30 seconds. Add tomatoes and ¼ cup parsley; reduce heat, and simmer 10 minutes. Add shrimp, and cook 5 minutes. Pour mixture into a 13- x 9-inch baking dish; sprinkle

STEP BY STEP: REMOVING LOBSTER MEAT

Plunge live lobster into 3 quarts boiling water; return to boil. Cover, reduce heat, and simmer 10 minutes. Lobster will turn red when done.

Remove walking legs; harvest meat from legs and cavities where legs attach. Twist lobster tail to remove it from the body.

Twist off the claws. Crack them with a nutcracker or mallet; carefully remove the meat.

Remove flippers from end of tail with kitchen shears. Insert your thumb where the flippers were attached and push the meat out of the opposite end.

with cheese. Bake at 400° for 10 minutes. Sprinkle with remaining parsley, juice, and pepper. Yield: 6 servings.

POINTS: 4; **Exchanges:** 3 Veg, ½ Med-Fat Meat, 1½ Very Lean Meat, ½ Fat
Per serving: CAL 191 (31% from fat); PRO 19.9g; FAT 6.5g (sat 3.2g, mono 1.7g, poly 1g); CARB 14.4g; FIB 2.1g; CHOL 125mg; IRON 3.8mg; SOD 752mg; CALC 211mg

Mackerel With Mint Vinaigrette

4   (6-ounce) mackerel fillets
Cooking spray
¼ cup red wine vinegar
1   teaspoon dried mint flakes
2   teaspoons olive oil
½ teaspoon dried rosemary
¼ teaspoon salt
¼ teaspoon pepper
2   large garlic cloves, finely chopped

1. Place mackerel, skin side down, on a broiler pan coated with cooking spray. Combine vinegar and next 6 ingredients; stir well. Brush half of vinegar mixture over fillets. Broil 6 minutes or until fish flakes easily when tested with a fork, basting with remaining vinegar mixture after 3 minutes. Yield: 4 servings.

POINTS: 5; **Exchanges:** 4½ Lean Meat
Per serving: CAL 228 (41% from fat); PRO 30.2g; FAT 10.5g (sat 2.6g); CARB 1.2g; FIB 0.1g; CHOL 93mg; IRON 1.1mg; SOD 231mg; CALC 22mg

Creamed Scallops, Corn, and Tomatoes

1   tablespoon margarine
1   cup sliced green onions
1½ pounds bay scallops
2   tablespoons all-purpose flour
1   teaspoon dried basil
½ teaspoon salt
½ teaspoon dried thyme
Dash to ¼ teaspoon ground red pepper
1½ cups frozen whole-kernel corn, thawed
½ cup whole milk
1   (14.5-ounce) can diced tomatoes, drained

1. Melt margarine over medium-high heat in a large nonstick skillet. Add green onions and scallops, and sauté 3 minutes. Add flour and next

4 ingredients, stirring until blended. Stir in corn, milk, and diced tomatoes; bring mixture to a boil, and cook 2 minutes or until slightly thick, stirring constantly. Yield: 4 servings (serving size: 1¼ cups).

POINTS: 6; **Exchanges:** 1½ Starch, 1 Veg, 1 Fat, 3½ Very Lean Meat
Per serving: CAL 301 (17% from fat); FAT 5.8g (sat 1.5g, mono 1.7g, poly 1.5g); PRO 33.5g; CARB 30.7g; FIB 3.5g; CHOL 60mg; IRON 7.8mg; SOD 797mg; CALC 220mg

Seafood Lasagna Florentine

½ cup all-purpose flour
2   cups 2% reduced-fat milk
¼ teaspoon salt
¼ teaspoon ground nutmeg
⅛ teaspoon ground red pepper
⅛ teaspoon black pepper
1   large garlic clove, crushed
¼ cup dry white wine
⅔ cup grated Parmesan cheese, divided
1   pound bay scallops
½ cup chopped fresh basil
1   tablespoon lemon juice
½ pound lump crabmeat, drained and shell pieces removed
1   large egg, lightly beaten
9   cooked lasagna noodles
2   (10-ounce) packages frozen chopped spinach, thawed, drained, and squeezed dry
½ teaspoon paprika

1. Preheat oven to 350°.

2. Place flour in a shallow baking pan. Bake at 350° for 30 minutes or until lightly browned, stirring after 15 minutes. Spoon flour into a large saucepan; gradually add milk, stirring with a whisk until blended. Stir in salt and next 4 ingredients, and cook over medium heat 5 minutes or until mixture is thick, stirring constantly. Add wine, and cook 1 minute, stirring constantly. Remove from heat; stir in ½ cup Parmesan cheese and scallops. Let cool slightly; stir in basil and next 3 ingredients. Increase oven temperature to 400°.

3. Spoon ¼ cup seafood sauce into bottom of a 13- x 9-inch baking dish. Arrange 3 lasagna

noodles in a single layer over seafood sauce, and top with one-third spinach; spoon one-third seafood sauce over spinach. Repeat layers, ending with seafood sauce. Combine remaining Parmesan cheese and paprika; stir well. Sprinkle cheese mixture over lasagna. Cover and bake at 400° for 30 minutes. Bake, uncovered, an additional 10 minutes. Let stand 10 minutes before serving. Yield: 9 servings.

POINTS: 6; **Exchanges:** 2½ Very Lean Meat, 1 Veg
Per serving: CAL 286 (16% from fat); PRO 24.8g; FAT 5.1g(sat 2.2g); CARB 33.6g; FIB 2.9g; CHOL 75mg; IRON 3.3mg; SOD 411mg; CALC 271mg

Sautéed Scallops on Lemon Fettuccine

¼ cup all-purpose flour
½ teaspoon salt
½ teaspoon cracked pepper
1 pound sea scallops
2 teaspoons olive oil

2 teaspoons margarine
⅓ cup vodka or dry white wine
1 teaspoon grated lemon rind
3 tablespoons fresh lemon juice
1 garlic clove, minced
6 cups hot cooked fettuccine (about 12 ounces uncooked)
¼ cup (1 ounce) finely grated fresh Parmesan cheese
¼ cup chopped fresh flat-leaf parsley

1. Combine flour, salt, and pepper in a large zip-top plastic bag. Add scallops; seal bag, and shake to coat.

2. Heat olive oil and margarine in a large non-stick skillet over high heat. Add scallops, and cook 2 minutes on each side or until lightly browned and done. Remove scallops from skillet; set aside, and keep warm. Reduce heat to medium; add vodka, lemon rind, lemon juice, and minced garlic; cook 3 minutes, stirring occasionally. Remove from heat; add fettuccine, and toss

Browning the flour in Seafood Lasagna Florentine gives the sauce a nutty flavor.

gently to coat. Divide pasta mixture evenly among 4 individual plates, and top with scallops. Sprinkle each serving with 1 tablespoon Parmesan cheese and 1 tablespoon chopped parsley. Yield: 4 servings.

POINTS: 9; **Exchanges:** 3 Very Lean Meat, 4 Starch, 1 Fat **Per serving:** CAL 481 (14% from fat); PRO 30.6g; FAT 7.3g (sat1.6, mono 3g, poly 1.7g); CARB 63.5; FIB 3.6g; CHOL 40mg; IRON 3.8mg; SOD 559mg; CALC 96mg

Chile-Rubbed Grilled-Scallop Salad

½   cup fresh lime juice
3   tablespoons sugar
2   tablespoons finely chopped unsalted, dry-roasted peanuts
2   tablespoons fish sauce
1   tablespoon peeled minced fresh ginger
3   garlic cloves, minced
2   tablespoons seeded finely chopped serrano chile
1   tablespoon cracked pepper
1½ pounds sea scallops
Cooking spray

8   cups coarsely chopped napa (Chinese) cabbage
2   cups red bell pepper strips
½   cup finely chopped fresh basil
½   cup minced fresh cilantro
⅓   cup finely chopped fresh mint

1. Combine first 6 ingredients; stir well, and set aside. Combine chile and cracked pepper; rub chile mixture onto scallops. Thread scallops onto each of 4 (12-inch) skewers.

2. Prepare grill. Place kabobs on grill rack coated with cooking spray; grill 4 minutes on each side or until scallops are done. Set aside; let cool slightly.

3. Combine cabbage, bell pepper, basil, cilantro, and mint in a bowl. Add lime juice mixture; toss well. Place 2 cups cabbage mixture on each of 4 plates; top each with 1 kabob. Yield: 4 servings.

POINTS: 5; **Exchanges:** 4 Very Lean Meat, 2 Veg, 1 Starch **Per serving:** CAL 267 (15% from fat); PRO 33.2g; FAT 4.4g (sat 0.6g); CARB 25.9g; FIB 3.5g; CHOL 56mg; IRON 3.4mg; SOD 1,403mg; CALC 230mg

Some like it hot, some like it cool. You'll get both sensations in this Chile-Rubbed Grilled-Scallop Salad.

Nutrition and Serving-Size Information

Here are some specific guidelines *Weight Watchers* Magazine adheres to regarding our recipes. For nutritional accuracy, please follow our suggestions.

• When preparing a recipe that yields more than one serving, it is important to mix the ingredients well and then divide the mixture evenly.

• Where liquid and solid parts have to be divided evenly, drain the liquid and set it aside. Evenly divide the remaining ingredients; then add equal amounts of the liquid to each serving.

• Unless otherwise indicated, selections of meat, poultry, and fish refer to cooked, skinned, and boned servings.

• The selection information is designated as follows: P/M (Protein/Milk), FA (Fat), FR/V (Fruit/Vegetable), B (Bread), C (Bonus Calories).

• The selection information no longer contains fractions: B, FR/V, and FA are rounded up if 0.5 or above; P/M is rounded up if 0.75 or above; and C only includes bonus calories above 30. If all of the selections are rounded up, bonus calories are decreased; if all of the selections are rounded down, bonus calories are increased.

• Recipes also provide approximate nutritional data, including the following: cal (calories), pro (protein), fat (total fat), sat (saturated fat), carb (carbohydrates), fib (dietary fiber), chol (cholesterol), iron (iron), sod (sodium), calc (calcium). Measurements are abbreviated as follows: g (grams), mg (milligrams).

Note: Because data on fat distribution are not available for some processed foods, these breakdowns should be considered approximate.

• Recipes include *POINTS*™ based on Weight Watchers International's 1•2•3 Success™ Weight Loss Plan. (Please turn to page 3 for more information about this plan.)

• *POINTS* are calculated from a formula based on calories, fat, and fiber that assigns higher points to higher-calorie, higher-fat foods. Based on your present weight, you are allowed a certain amount of *POINTS* per day.

• The recipes that are shown in our photographs may vary as to the number of servings pictured. It is important that you refer to the recipes for the exact serving information.

USEFUL EQUIVALENTS FOR LIQUID INGREDIENTS BY VOLUME

	Fahrenheit	Celsius	Gas Mark
Freeze Water	32° F	0°C	
Room Temperature	68° F	20° C	
Boil Water	212° F	100° C	
Bake	325° F	160° C	3
	350° F	180° C	4
	375° F	190° C	5
	400° F	200° C	6
	425° F	220° C	7
	450° F	230° C	8
Broil			Grill

RECIPE INDEX